Perfectly WEIRD, Perfectly YOU

The library is always open at
renfrewshirelibraries.co.uk

Visit now for
homework help
and free
eBooks.

SKOOBS

We are the Skoobs and we love the library!

Phone: 0300 300 1188
Email: libraries@renfrewshire.gov.uk

Perfectly WEIRD, Perfectly YOU

A SCIENTIFIC GUIDE TO GROWING UP

CAMILLA PANG

ILLUSTRATED BY LAURÈNE BOGLIO

wren
&rook

FOR TIGER RAMSEY, LILLY PANG,
AGATHA PANG

First published in Great Britain in 2022 by Wren & Rook
ISBN: 978 1 5263 6432 6
E-book ISBN: 978 1 5263 6433 3

1 3 5 7 9 10 8 6 4 2

MIX
Paper from
responsible sources
FSC® C104740

FSC
www.fsc.org

Wren & Rook
An imprint of
Hachette Children's Group
Part of Hodder & Stoughton
Carmelite House
50 Victoria Embankment
London EC4Y 0DZ

An Hachette UK Company
www.hachette.co.uk
www.hachettechildrens.co.uk

Printed and bound in Great Britain by Clays Ltd, Elcograf S.p.A.

INTRODUCTION

My name is Dr Camilla Pang.
But you can call me Millie.

I want to start by telling you
something important about me.
I have always been a bit weird.
Actually, quite a lot **WEIRD**.

I was the one in class who always
put up their hand, but used to get
flustered if a teacher picked me
out to ask a question.

I always had my nose in a book,
but I'd also get bored during
lessons and be told off for
staring out of the window.

And I always tried to be polite,
but quite often ended up saying
something a bit rude by accident.

I'm still pretty weird today.

I get massively **EXCITED** about things,
to the point where I can't stop my body from
shaking or I make little squeaking noises.

But sometimes I get so scared that I have to hide under my duvet cover or sit under my desk until I feel safe again. (I am twenty-eight years old.)

There's a lot about me that doesn't really make sense. In fact, these are probably my favourite parts of myself. We are all human beings, not robots, and we are all different – weird in our special, sometimes illogical way.

But, as I discovered when I was eight years old, I was different from most people in one particular way. This is when I was diagnosed with autism spectrum disorder, ASD for short.

Autism can be difficult to explain, because everyone on the autistic spectrum experiences it in a different way.

But I'll have a go anyway (with apologies to my fellow ASD crew who may not recognise these things in their own lives).

In *general*, autism can mean:

⚛ Having very **STRONG** feelings that you struggle to explain to other people.

⚛ Feeling **OVERWHELMED** by the five senses. Bright colours, nasty smells, strange textures, unfamiliar tastes and loud noises can scare or unsettle you so much that they send your whole body and brain into meltdown.

Finding it **DIFFICULT** to understand people's body language and tone of voice (e.g. when someone raises their eyebrows or speaks in a sarcastic or angry way, you might not 'get' the message).

Having very specific **ROUTINES** to live by, to stop yourself from doing everything in the wrong order (like leaving the house before getting dressed properly, or trying to eat a meal you haven't cooked yet).

Relying on little quirks of **BEHAVIOUR** (called tics) to feel safe and calm, most of which are about soothing the senses. These might include repeating the same words over and over, following a routine very closely or making sudden, jerky movements with your head and hands. The repetition of words or movements like this is known as 'stimming' (self-stimulation).

These are just a few of the ways people with autism may behave differently, and they are based on my experience (which may not reflect or represent anyone else's).

For some people with ASD, autism will define and sometimes limit their lives in a major way. For others, it will not make too much difference.

I'm somewhere in between. My ASD meant that I was often confused and scared while growing up. I had to work harder than most people to understand the world and find my place in it. Because lots of people doubted me, I had to learn to stand up for myself and to believe in who I was and what I had to offer the world.

I'd spend so long looking at how people moved their hands when talking, hoping it would give me a clue about my place in the conversation, that I sometimes forgot to listen to what they were saying.

And I had lots of people looking at me strangely and calling me a weirdo for making my strange noises or saying things that didn't really make sense.

That makes my childhood sound difficult, and sometimes it was.

But I don't regret having ASD, not even a little bit.

In fact, I think of it as my **SUPERPOWER**.
And I'm grateful for it.

Because, while I might struggle to do things many people find easy (like making plans at the last minute, or talking to someone I've never met before), I can also do things they can't.

My ASD makes me **BRAVE** in ways that lots of people aren't. When I see something strange or wrong, I will point it out before I've thought about whether this might be rude or 'impolite'. That *can* lead to some difficult situations, but it also means I'm more likely to say the thing that needs saying, when other people are too embarrassed to mention it.

It also makes me a bit obsessive about things, which is incredibly useful for learning. When I get interested in something, I will drop everything and spend all my time reading about it, sometimes for several days in a row. This was how I got interested in science in the first place, and it's how I still am today.

And most importantly, my ASD makes me **CURIOUS**. I've had to learn almost everything about living in this world the same way everyone else learns to swim or memorises the names of capital cities.

I didn't just 'pick up' the ability to make friends, say the right thing or read other people's body language. I've had to **STUDY** all these things, really thinking about how they work and devising my own formulas and shortcuts.

Put another way, I've had to be a scientist my whole life. I've been studying people, watching their behaviour and making notes – all to help me work out how *I* could belong in a place that has often felt like another planet.

And now, aged twenty-eight and with some cool letters before and after my name that mean I'm now a doctor, I'm here to share with you what I learned – and why I think it might help you too.

SCIEN-TASTIC

I already told you one important thing about me. There's a second too. I love science. **LOVE** science.

Aged ten, I saw a copy of *New Scientist* magazine in a newsagent while shopping with my mum. I started reading an article about a serious medical problem – the sort of thing that would normally have terrified me for the rest of the day.

But then I realised that the story was about what scientists were doing to *solve* this problem. And I knew right then that I always wanted to be the first to know how science could make the world better and safer. I scraped together my pocket money to start buying the magazine, and I've loved it ever since. Now instead of worrying about something that makes me afraid, I always ask myself: can I do something about it? That has been science's gift to me.

When other kids my age had posters of pop stars or footballers on their walls, I clung to my favourite book by Stephen Hawking (one of the most legendary scientists of the last century – look him up!).

It was one of many books that I devoured about the chemistry, physics and biology that make our world tick.

So much of the 'real' world around me didn't make sense: the words that people said, the expressions on their faces or the things they seemed to expect me to do without ever actually asking.

But the scientific world of my beloved books was beautiful and logical. There were *systems* with *rules* that I could learn by heart, which fitted together neatly in my head like LEGO bricks.

17

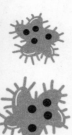

I loved reading about the different bits of the body, the way plants generate their own food and how our universe first came into being.

As I grew up, science started to become my guide for a world that felt scary and confusing.

It was easier for me to understand why a plant wanted to move towards the sunlight, than why my sister always turned up the volume when her favourite singer, Peter Andre, came on the radio.

It was easier for me to understand the forces that control our world (like gravity, which makes things fall down, or magnetism, which draws them together), than it was to recognise the forces that sometimes exist between people (like friendship and peer pressure).

And it was easier for me to understand how metals react with the liquids and gases around them, than how humans make friends with some people but not with others.

Gradually, I learned to use the stuff I could understand – the **TANGIBLE, LOGICAL** and **BEAUTIFUL** patterns of science – to help translate everything around me that I *couldn't* understand: the **STRANGE, MESSY** and **CONFUSING** world of humans.

I learned that the science behind the weather could teach me about human emotions – how they can change so quickly from the happiness of a sunny day to the meltdown or temper tantrum of a thunderstorm.

I learned from computers to have confidence in my need to question everything around me – and discovered that doing this can lead to better, more complete answers.

And I learned, from the way our entire body grows out of one single stem cell, that if you want to achieve anything important, then you *really* have to work at it – to keep going and going, just like the body does.

Over time, the science that I discovered became my personal guidebook to life.

And now I'm sharing it with you.

In the chapters that follow, we're going to look at some of the hardest and most important parts of life – from managing emotions to handling disagreements, from pursuing your passions to understanding your relationships with other people.

And we're going to use a different bit of science to explain and explore each of them.

Now, I realise that people can feel *strongly* about science. Maybe, like me, it's your favourite subject at school. Or perhaps it's the one you really **DON'T** look forward to.

Whether you fall into one of these groups, or somewhere in between, I hope you'll follow me on this journey. And I hope I can give you a different way of thinking about science.

Because science doesn't live in the classroom or sleep in the lab. It's all around us, in everything we see, say, think and touch. It's the fabric of our world: a beautiful, fascinating subject that everyone deserves the chance to understand, appreciate and enjoy.

It's incredibly important too: the only way to explain baffling things that otherwise don't make sense.

Science was my guidebook to life, and I want to show how it can give you a new way of looking at yours, too.

BECOMING YOURSELF

My love and need for science was one of the products of my ASD. Another was that I had to work **REALLY** hard to understand myself: the person I wanted to be and the life I wanted to have.

20

When people are giving you strange looks and calling you nasty names – which unfortunately happened a lot to me – it's easy to lose confidence in yourself. You question the way you behave and the things you enjoy.

Overcoming that doubt has been one of the biggest achievements of my life. It's allowed me to become the person I am, and to be proud of the things that make me different, things which have given me a unique view of the world and helped me to fulfil my dream of a life working in science.

I think it's the same for all of us. It's really **HARD** learning to be yourself: to do the things that interest you, find the friends you really chime with and have the confidence not to change your mind just because other people are trying to make you. But it's also one of the most rewarding things you will ever do.

And it's something that you have to do for yourself; no one else can do it for you. Because we are all different. We all see and experience the world in a slightly different way (and some of us in a *very* different way). We all have our own strange little behaviours, likes and dislikes, and things that make us afraid. We are **ALL** weird, in our own wonderful and unique way.

The hard part of growing up is working this out: learning who you are as a person, having confidence

in your own instincts and understanding what actually makes you happy (as opposed to what other people like or what happens to be popular that week).

It's about having the courage to be yourself and to feel safe standing out from the crowd, as well as finding ways to blend in.

That's what this book is about. I've written it to help you **BELIEVE** in yourself, cope with things that make you afraid, stand up to peer pressure, pursue your passions and find true friends.

It's about all the things you **CAN** do to discover and become your awesome self. The person that only **YOU** can be. And the only person you should ever **WANT** to be.

Growing up isn't easy. But science, which has an explanation for most things, can be our guide. If you've ever wondered why metal can dissolve in water, how we grow our toenails or where polar bears go on their summer holidays, then read on.

We'll learn some things about the world. Even more importantly, we'll learn about **OURSELVES**.

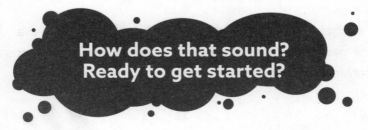

How does that sound? Ready to get started?

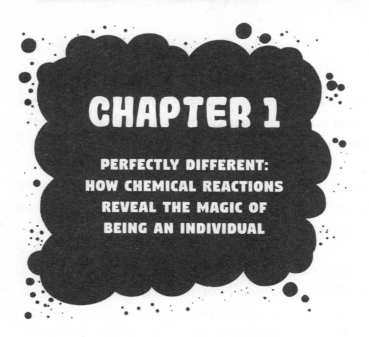

CHAPTER 1

PERFECTLY DIFFERENT: HOW CHEMICAL REACTIONS REVEAL THE MAGIC OF BEING AN INDIVIDUAL

This story begins in my school playground, during lunch break, eighteen years ago.

Not long before the bell was due to go, I saw a girl I didn't know very well, wearing a pair of blue trainers I immediately liked.

Often, I don't notice or really care about clothes (unless they poke or itch me, or the colour scares me), but I couldn't stop looking at these trainers.

Feeling warm inside with excitement, I walked up to her. 'Cool shoes. I might get them too!'

Blue trainers girl looked at me like she'd just sniffed a bottle of milk that had gone bad. The bridge of her nose crinkled and the sides of her mouth turned down.

'Don't you dare copy me,' she said. And when I asked why, she smiled with thin lips. 'No offence, but people like *you* don't hang around with people like *me*.'

Because, at the age of ten, I didn't understand when people were trying to be mean to me (or why they might want to be), I wasn't upset. I didn't know that she was trying to insult me. But I was confused. I didn't see what trainers had to do with anything except putting something comfy and shiny on your feet.

When people did or said things that confused me, a sound would sometimes go off in my head like a trumpet. At that moment, I could hear a whole orchestra playing. The look on her face and the words coming out of her mouth seemed out of tune: discordant and harsh.

And as the trumpet blared in my mind, I felt like a hundred questions were being shouted in my ear. Why would two girls, of the same age, at the same school, not be able to hang out together? What did she mean by 'people like you'? Were there really different 'types' of people? And can we all be put in a box depending on the things we like, the way we are, how we look and the kind of shoes we wear?

STEREOTYPES ARE SILLY

That short conversation had left me with lots of questions, and all this time later I still haven't answered some of them. The strange magic of what makes people want to be friends with each other is something no one can fully explain. It's never as simple as going to the same school, liking the same things or even choosing to wear the same kind of shoes.

People who seem to be completely different from each other, in every way you could think of, can be the best of friends and get similar grades. And others who seem to have everything in common, to be the same 'type' (in this case having the same trainer preferences), might not get on at all.

In other words, we can't know everything about someone based only on the 'type' of person we think they are. You don't always know how someone is going to behave just because they like football or always put up their hand in class. When we judge people based on how we expect them to behave – because of how they look or how they are – we are **STEREOTYPING**, assuming that everyone of that 'type' will think and behave in the same way.

Here are some stereotypes ...

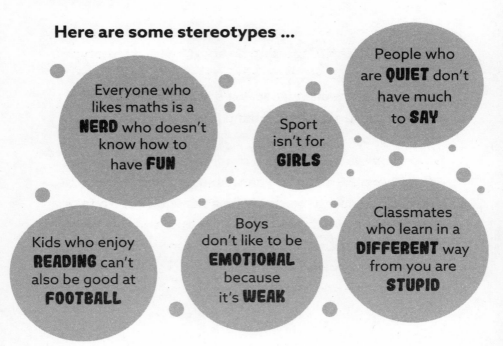

Everyone who likes maths is a **NERD** who doesn't know how to have **FUN**

People who are **QUIET** don't have much to **SAY**

Sport isn't for **GIRLS**

Kids who enjoy **READING** can't also be good at **FOOTBALL**

Boys don't like to be **EMOTIONAL** because it's **WEAK**

Classmates who learn in a **DIFFERENT** way from you are **STUPID**

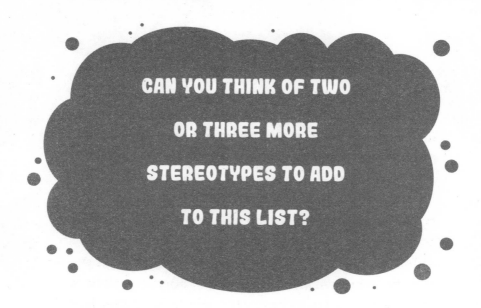

CAN YOU THINK OF TWO OR THREE MORE STEREOTYPES TO ADD TO THIS LIST?

CLEARLY, stereotypes aren't helpful! (And, in case you were wondering, all of the above are completely untrue.)

By pretending that we can know everything about a person based on just *one* thing about them, stereotyping simplifies all the small, important bits that make every single one of us an individual. It's like trying to squeeze a whole person, and everything they contain, into a matchbox.

Much worse, stereotypes can also do harm. They can be a way for people to discriminate against others (to treat them worse than they would someone else), or even themselves, because of what the stereotype is telling them to think or do.

A stereotype about people with autism, like me, is that we can't make friends. That we are rude, are oversensitive, will always behave weirdly, are embarrassing to know and won't be able to get a job when we grow up.

My life proves that none of those things are true: I have the two jobs I always dreamed of, as a scientist and a writer. I have lots of friends and a life I love, and most importantly I have learned to be **PROUD** of myself, to **EMBRACE** every quirk and bit of weirdness that makes me Millie.

Yet despite all of these things, I know that everyone who meets me and knows about my condition will be thinking about autism stereotypes before they have even spoken to me.

For some people I am too strange to be considered **'NORMAL'**, and for others I seem too normal for them to believe that I am autistic (and yes, I do sometimes get asked whether I am or not). *That* is the problem with stereotypes.

> They make us treat people as we EXPECT them to be, not as they actually ARE.

When you are on the receiving end of this, it can make you question who you really are, and if the stereotype has any value.

No one should ever be judged based on how they look, the things that make them different or the interests they have.

But that isn't the same thing as saying that there aren't different types of people. Some of us like to be in a crowded room full of people chatting, while others prefer small groups and quieter settings. Some people love to be outdoors, tramping about in the rain and the mud, while others like to be curled up inside where it's warm and dry. Some people thrive on trying new things and meeting new people, while others like the comforts of home and what they are most familiar with. And still more people enjoy a mixture of both!

As long as we don't stereotype – assume that because we know *one* thing about a person, we automatically know *everything* about them – then types can sometimes be quite useful. They are a way to begin (but only *begin*) understanding ourselves and other people.

I didn't know this when I walked up to that girl in the playground and said that I liked her shoes. And I walked away from that conversation with thoughts buzzing around my head like flies, feeling restless and like every part of me was itching. **People like me. People like you.** Were we really so different, and did it matter? I knew I had to find out.

HEAVY METAL

To my ten-year-old self, humans were a mystery. And to be honest with you, writing this now, aged twenty-eight, they often still are! To understand something as complicated as personality type, I was going to need help. Is it something you can hold, hear, see or smell?

So I looked for something that could help me. Something solid, reliable and almost as interesting as people themselves.

And I found **METAL**.

Now, I can almost hear you asking as you read this: what has **METAL** got to do with *me*?! It's a fair question. Because it isn't immediately obvious what the stuff we make frying pans out of and build bridges from could tell us about people.

On the surface, an inanimate object like metal, one that can't talk or roll its eyes at you, shouldn't have much to say about humans and the millions of little things that form our personalities.

But scratch that surface or tap on that bike frame, and a different story starts to emerge. Because while we might think metals are all similar – strong and tough – they actually *behave* very differently.

There are metals that you can cut like a piece of cake with a knife from the kitchen drawer, and metals that fizz and dissolve when you put them in water. Some will even **EXPLODE** when they come into contact with water. Others are so flammable they can light up when you *breathe* on them.

Metals are also adaptable, doing different things in different forms. For example, when sodium is a crystal, it forms part of the salt you put on food, but when it is a gas, it helps to light up street lamps at night. Metals: more flexible than you thought!

Some metals are good when you need something strong and durable. Others are best if you want the kind of sparks and explosions you get in a firework display.

And the secret to why metals behave differently, and why they are good at different things, is their **REACTIVITY**.

Reactivity simply means how likely (or not) an element is to take part in a chemical reaction. These reactions are happening all around us, every second of the day. They are happening inside our bodies, in the kitchen when we cook a meal, every time we use soap to wash our hands, and when we breathe, laugh, cry, shout and get tickled.

In fact, our whole existence is based on one very important chemical reaction, known as respiration. This is when the air we breathe combines with the glucose we get from food, generating the energy we need for the body to function (and creating carbon dioxide and water in the process – we'll return to those in chapter 5).

Chemical reactions may be everywhere, but that doesn't mean everything is equally likely to be reactive. Which brings us back to metals, and types. Just like there are different personality types in humans, there are different **TYPES** of metals that react in their own particular ways. Let's have a look at how they work and what their reactivity can tell us about our own personalities.

PASTA-NALITY

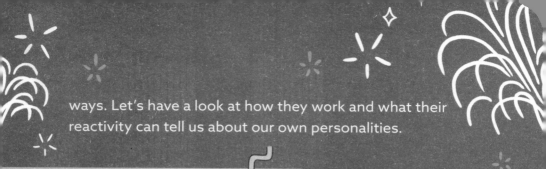

Let's say you are having pasta for lunch. You fill up a pan with water, you heat up that water on the hob and, if you're being fancy, you dissolve salt into the boiling water to make it taste good. This is how it is done in Italy, after all.

All sorts of reactions are happening. For a start, it's a chemical reaction known as combustion (the fancy word for burning) that produces the strange blue light we use to cook on a gas hob.

But that's not all. There are two other reactions to interest us here: one that is happening very *quickly*, and another that is occurring extremely *slowly*.

Let's start with the quick one. When you pour salt (technically, sodium chloride) into boiling water, the salt dissolves because the chemical bond holding its two parts (sodium and chlorine) together is pulled apart. This happens almost instantly because the water is hot, with the temperature acting as a **CATALYST** for the reaction (something that makes it go faster).

Now go back a step. When you (or a responsible adult) filled up the pan, the water that came out of the kitchen tap had to travel through lots of pipes snaking around your house. There's a good chance that these pipes are made out of copper, and there's an equally good reason.

Because, whereas sodium (as found in table salt) is one of the most reactive metals, copper is near the bottom of that league table. It is much *less* reactive, which makes it excellent for the job of having lots and lots of water flow through it every day. That's because when metals come into contact with water, they react with the oxygen in it and undergo a chemical reaction called **OXIDATION**. This is what makes some metals turn rusty or get damaged, like the bits on your bike that go brown and flaky when left out in the rain one night too many. They have become iron oxide, otherwise known as rust.

The benefit of copper is that it reacts very *slowly* with the oxygen in water, meaning it takes a very long time to be affected by oxidation. (Which isn't to say it doesn't react eventually. Over long periods of time, it can turn green. Like the Statue of Liberty, which is made of copper and was originally brown.)

This **LACK** of reactivity is just one of the reasons copper is such a useful metal for making pipes that we need to last. It can do its job for a long, long time without being

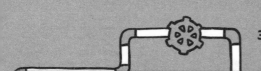

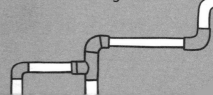

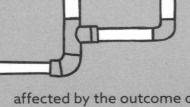

affected by the outcome of chemical reactions. If we made the same pipes out of iron, the oxidation reaction would create rust that would flake off and turn your pasta water a reddish-brown colour. **UGH**.

The same logic explains why the even less reactive metals (silver, gold and platinum) are the ones used in jewellery – because they won't turn a funny colour even after years and years of being exposed to oxygen while sitting on your finger or hanging from your ears. And if you've ever worn a piece of jewellery that turned your skin a bit green, you'll know why: it's part copper!

But back to pasta. The simple act of cooking that meal shows us two different ends of the reactivity spectrum. An element (sodium) that we rely on to be *reactive* and make everything taste delicious, and another (copper) that we need to be *unreactive* to keep our water safe when travelling around the house.

The moral of the story? Both the most and least reactive elements are important in different ways, because they are good at different things and work together in ways that enable us to cook, eat our favourite foods, watch TV, phone our friends, write and breathe at the same time.

As I'll now explain, I think the same is true of us as people.

WE'RE PEOPLE, NOT PERSONALITIES

If you're trying to understand why we are all different from each other, there's one thing to know first. Which is that, in biological terms, we are almost identical – up to **99.9%** made of the same human building blocks, which scientists call DNA.

So all the differences between us – whether we are tall or short, have brown or green eyes, have skin of a particular colour, are good at sport or can't catch a ball to save our life – are packed into just **0.1%** of the biological ingredients that we are made of.

All the things that we spend our time thinking about, from the shoes we wear to the bits of our parents we have inherited, are just a drop in the ocean of who we actually are. Even if we look, sound, think or behave differently from the person next to us, those differences are dwarfed by how similar we all are as human beings.

I didn't know this when the girl in the blue trainers told me that people 'like me' couldn't hang out with people 'like her'. But I did know, through instinct, that I was bigger than the matchbox she was trying to put me in. I knew that her belief that the trainers would become weird or uncool if I wore them couldn't really be true.

She was being unfair. She had decided what she thought about me before she had even got to know me (not very nice or scientific). And she was focusing not on the 99.9% that we had in common, but the 0.1% of differences that she could see: all the small ways I didn't fit into her view of how someone should behave.

She showed me that, unfortunately, there are some people who find differences uncomfortable. They want other people to agree with them and to look and talk like them. They think different equals weird. They don't know that you can cut some metals with a butter knife. And they are **WRONG**!

Because what metals and reactivity taught me is that difference isn't a bad thing. It's a good one, because we can't survive if everyone is the same. We need people to be good at different things, to react differently, otherwise we would all be bad at the same things. If every metal was as reactive as sodium, then our world would crumble and fall apart around us. Imagine, no more pasta!

I think it's the same with people. Some of us are like the more reactive metals when added to water. If you put us in a crowd of people we don't know, we will fizz and pop with the excitement of getting to know everyone. People like this can't have enough conversations; they can never meet enough new people.

Whereas someone who is quieter by nature, who feels more comfortable with people they already know, may not react. Like a piece of copper put into that same water, nothing will happen.

Others are somewhere in between. They stay quiet and observe a situation, even though they might have something to say. Some days they have the confidence and interest to speak up, and others they don't.

These differences are what make us human, and a big part of what makes life so interesting. A lesson wouldn't work if every member of the class wanted to speak the whole time or if no one ever put up their hand. A sports team would fall apart if everyone tried to shout instructions at the same time. And fashion would become *extremely* boring if we all agreed on what to wear and no one ever tried anything different. Almost as if we would all be in uniform! (Oh wait ...)

We need **DIFFERENCE** in our world. Differences are what make life interesting and full of flavour. They are something to embrace and should never be used as a basis to judge someone or think badly of them. Remember that what someone thinks of you is just their opinion, not a fact. There is only one person who gets to decide who you should be, and that's **YOU**.

How much do these differences define us as people? Are we limited to being one 'type' of person, always behaving the same way? **NO!** Because the other thing metals teach us is that the **CONTEXT** matters. Reactivity depends on the metal, but also on the conditions it encounters – like the temperature at which it melts or freezes, or what kind of liquid it has come into contact with.

In people terms, this means someone who might be quiet in one environment could be very chatty in another where they feel safer with friends they know well. And someone who might lack confidence in one area could be full of it in another.

In the end, it's all about finding the environment in which you feel happiest and most comfortable: the one in which *you* will be reactive.

I met the blue trainers girl again at a birthday party and beat her at Mario Kart. She was full of confidence in the playground (her natural environment) but not at all when it came to a head-to-head competition online (which was mine).

The mistake that girl made – other than challenging me at Mario Kart – was that she tried to **JUDGE** me before she even knew me. She decided what type of person I was, and that we were never going to be friends, almost before we had actually met. She never stopped to **THINK** that we might just be reactive (and cool) in different environments.

Personality types are real and they have their uses. It's a good way of starting to understand yourself and the people in your life. But it's *only* the beginning. Type can never tell us everything, because we are all individuals – and individuals are as likely to break the 'rules' of their personality type as to follow them, especially when we are growing up and learning. Just like metals, which, as we've seen, can behave very differently in different states.

Someone who is quiet in class might be the first person to step forward and sing in the choir. Someone else who seems full of confidence might be terrified of something you find easy, like putting their head underwater during a swimming lesson.

That's where a friend steps in, giving someone the space to react and the support they need to deal with something difficult; not trying to flatten them like the trainer girl did to me.

Don't laugh at people for what they can't easily do, or even feel sorry for them. Instead, cheer them on, help them to feel like they can do something they are scared of, handle their reaction with care and hold their hand.

In the end, we are
PEOPLE,
not personality types.

We can never be fully explained by the boxes people want to put us in – like shy, loud, clever, confident, boisterous, weird, sensitive, athletic or bookish. These might explain part of what makes us tick, but they never get everything. They are small parts and not the whole.

Every one of us is too **INTERESTING**, too **INDIVIDUAL** and, yes, too **WEIRD**, to be defined in this way.

And that is the fun, exciting and unpredictable bit about being human. We react and it is the most beautiful thing in the world, where a single smile can feel like a firework exploding into the sky in all its colours and brightness.

It is by celebrating and encouraging difference, helping everyone to be themselves, that we **LIGHT** up all our **LIVES**.

CHAPTER 2

PERFECTLY CALM: HOW TO MANAGE YOUR EMOTIONS LIKE THE WEATHER

Sometimes, we all find it difficult to express how we really feel. To get people to understand why we're sad, what's making us laugh or what we actually want.

Emotions like these are such a **POWERFUL** thing, physically affecting our brain and body, that they can be hard to put into words.

I know how much I struggled to do this, and often still do. Whether I was excited by something or afraid of it, my feelings used to spill out of me like lava boiling over the edge of a volcano.

If someone asked me about my interests, I'd **BLURT** out every single one I could think of in full detail: so excited about what I had to say and how much I wanted them to hear it that I couldn't stop myself from saying everything at once. This was accompanied by dramatic arm movements, which put the people who had politely asked a question at risk of being whacked on the nose by my enthusiasm!

At other times, I wouldn't have any words at all, just a bubbling feeling that wanted to escape my body. Looking for a way to get rid of it, I sometimes tried copying my dog, Auckie, in the way he shook his head wildly after being out in the rain. I even tried mimicking the sounds of a kettle boiling, the water bubbling and steam escaping, in the hope these might help me to expel my own feelings and explain them.

The struggle to express and manage our emotions is something that we all face from the very beginning of our lives. As babies, we scream and cry because we have no other way of telling people that we are hungry, tired or stressed.

Even when we get older and learn to talk, sometimes words fail us and we get overwhelmed by tears, a hot feeling in our cheeks, a rapid heartbeat in our chests and even the need to kick or throw things.

We all have emotions, and they don't go away as we grow older. That's a good thing. Our ability to feel is one of the most important things that makes us human. It explains our ability to be passionate about our interests and pursue our dreams, and to love other people and comfort them when they are upset.

Strong emotions are one of the **BEST** parts of being alive. Like when we're laughing with a friend, when our team scores the winning goal, or when we read or watch something that immediately connects with us – and we know we want to experience it again and again.

But emotions can be overwhelming, and learning how to manage them is one of the most important parts of growing up. So in this chapter, we'll take a closer look. Why do we feel so strongly about things that they affect our entire body? How can we be more in control of our emotions than they are of us? And what can the favourite conversation topic of most grown-ups, the weather, teach us about **WHY** and **HOW** we feel?

THE COMPUTER IN YOUR HEAD

One thing I'm sure you all remember is what it feels like to throw a proper tantrum. To feel your emotions boiling over to the point where your body and mind seem to be acting outside your control. When everything shakes, your ears feel stuffed with sirens, your eyes feel drenched in vinegar and your stomach turns around and around like a washing machine.

We might feel a tantrum or meltdown in our eyes, face and tummy, but that isn't where it started. Like everything in the body, the brain is where it all begins.

So let's take a peek inside this human computer to find out more.

In particular, we need to know about two bits of the brain. The first is called the *amygdala* (a-mig-da-la), a funny thing shaped like an almond that behaves a bit like a smoke alarm.

The amygdala is responsible for keeping us safe by making the body aware of when it might be in danger. If we see someone with an angry look on their face, or an animal that might cause us harm, the amygdala is the first part of us that notices (so go on, give yourself a pat on the head).

And when it does, another part of the brain swings into action: the *hypothalamus* (hi-poe-thala-mus). This is a tiny part of the brain that's buried right in the middle. Despite its small stature, it's incredibly important. It takes the information coming from other parts of the

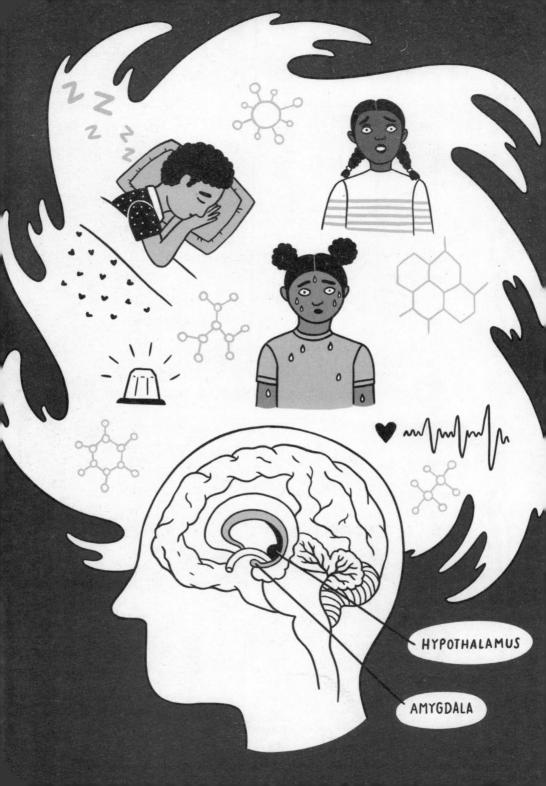

HYPOTHALAMUS

AMYGDALA

brain and decides how the body should respond. It is the boss of many different parts – a bit like the body's head teacher.

When we start sweating, sense our heart pounding or feel sleepy, we have the hypothalamus to thank (or to blame!). It is doing its job of controlling how the body behaves in relation to everything around it. The temperature of the body is a good example. When the weather gets too hot, our bodies need to lower their temperature, so we sweat. And when it's cold, the opposite happens and the hairs on our body 'stand up' to stop it from losing heat, forming goosebumps on our skin.

If it wasn't busy enough keeping us cool, the hypothalamus also has another essential job. It releases **HORMONES**, which are chemicals that tell organs in the body what to do. It's the hormones controlled by the hypothalamus that play a big part in making us feel **ANGRY, STRESSED** and **AFRAID**. Like adrenaline, the hormone that brings everything to life and fills you with rocket-like excitement!

So when we have that meltdown, it's because those two bits of our brain are whirring away to make us aware of something. The amygdala has spotted danger and the hypothalamus has responded – making our heart beat faster, increasing our blood pressure and making the muscles in our body go all tense. Our minds get rattled and anxious and often we cry, and blood pumps to our cheeks, which is why we go red and blotchy.

Our body has spotted danger – it is getting ready to fight it, and the stress of all this is what threatens to send us into an uncontrollable meltdown.

This response has deep roots in human nature, from the days when we lived in caves, hunted for food and were at risk of being eaten by wild animals.

At moments like these, the release of hormones, including our friend adrenaline, causes what is known as the **'FIGHT OR FLIGHT'** response. It's how we prepare to protect ourselves from the things that we think are dangerous. Either we decide to try and do battle with the animal (or maths exam) that is coming to eat us, or we run away from it. If you've ever had an argument with a brother or sister, then you know what the fight part looks like. And if you've ever stormed out of the room or run away in tears, well, that's flight.

So although being 'emotional' might seem like irrational behaviour, in many ways it makes complete sense. This ability to be sensitive is what has protected human beings for thousands of years. Our emotions are not just part of *being* alive. They are also essential to *staying* alive.

WHEN THE STORM ARRIVES

Now, all of you reading this are past what we might call prime tantrum age (*coughs at twenty-eight years old*). You probably don't scream, stamp your feet and bang your head on the wall when you get stressed (although maybe you do – I know I did, which is why I also know it doesn't work). But you may feel and do other things, like **FRUSTRATION**, which might make you argue with people, stomp out of the room or stop talking to your family altogether.

As we grow up, our ability to manage extreme emotions gets better over time. First we learn to communicate, whether it's using our body language, talking, writing or drawing. These methods allow us to express and get across our thoughts and feelings, helping other people (like parents, siblings, friends and teachers) to help us.

In brain terms we are developing too. Something called the frontal lobe, the part that does a lot of the brain's 'big' thinking (like making decisions or solving puzzles) grows *very* slowly. In fact, yours won't be fully developed until you're about twenty-five.

So the bit of the brain that acts as the voice of calm reason isn't completely ready to do that job until we're grown-ups. Only after we're done growing up does our body reach the point where it recognises that every new signal isn't an urgent one. Before that, we're still taking in everything new around us and reacting to most of it.

Even when the frontal lobe has developed, that doesn't stop us from feeling strong emotions in a way that can be hard to deal with.

We can't deny our emotions, so we have to find a way to put their energy to use, like when a puppy is being boisterous because it wants to be played with or taken for a walk. And if running around the room isn't your thing, talking can work too. Maybe you can ask a parent or older sibling how they deal with their feelings in difficult situations.

Everyone has their own different approach, but sometimes we can borrow tips or techniques that work for other people and try them out for ourselves. You might find it helpful to write down your feelings in a diary (which is helpful for venting on the day something happens, and later reminding us how quickly we can forget about things that we found angering or upsetting at the time). Or you could draw (which was a favourite approach of mine), expressing your emotions through pictures, helping to give form and shape to otherwise squishy feelings. I sometimes use an emotion wheel to help identify and recognise complicated feelings. I find the wheel useful when trying to understand and verbalise my emotions in certain situations, rather than relying on what people tell me to think or what I *should* feel.

FIND OUT THREE WAYS THAT OTHER PEOPLE DEAL WITH STRONG EMOTIONS IN THEIR LIFE. WRITE THEM DOWN SO THAT YOU CAN REFER TO THEM IN THE FUTURE.

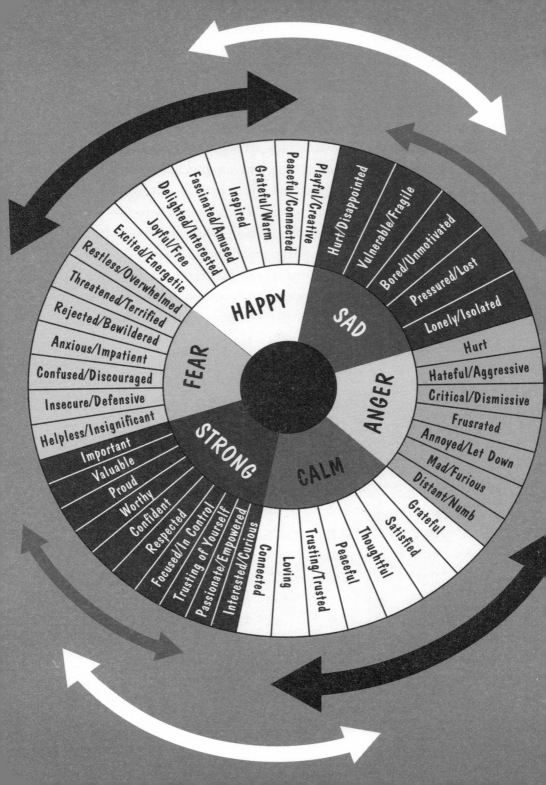

However we do it, the important thing is to find a way to deal with whatever makes us anxious or upset. We have to be ready for when the amygdala spots something it doesn't like and the warning lights start flashing.

Because if that happens and we're not ready for it, then there's a good chance that we fall into the grip of a full-scale meltdown: crying so hard that we can't even speak, or becoming so angry that we have to scream, making it impossible to think about anything else. We're not calm enough to think about the parts of our brain that are making us do this.

And this is where I think our friend the weather can help us.

AN EMOTIONAL UMBRELLA

Think about how rain happens. It's when the water droplets that have come together to form a cloud get bigger and bigger, until they're so heavy that they have to fall down. Sometimes you can feel the sky and the atmosphere heavy and ready for rain – to this day, it can make me feel nervous!

But, as you know, there are lots of different types of rain. There's a light drizzle that you walk through without thinking. And then there are heavy, horrible, pelting showers that leave us wet through. Sometimes you can see the rain building up for hours, as the clouds slowly get darker and darker. And on other days a blue sky can turn dark, or produce rain, almost without warning.

Our emotions are the same. Sometimes we *know* that we're about to do something that will make us anxious or afraid: like an exam or a piece of homework we might struggle with. And at other times, we get overwhelmed by something that happens without warning, like falling off our bike.

Of course, not all the emotional weather is rainy or stormy. Being with people who make you feel safe and happy, and doing things that you love, can make even the greyest Sunday afternoon feel like it is full of blazing sunshine. Whenever I think of my mum, I think of a day with blue skies so clear that you could see for miles, with flowers blooming all around.

Whether it's sunny, cloudy or stormy, the weather is one of the things in life that humans can't control. But we can be **READY** for it, prepared with an umbrella or experienced enough to know that one rain shower isn't the end of the world.

The role that emotions play in our lives is quite similar. Accidents and surprises can't be prepared for, but lots of other things can. Like the rain, it's a lot easier to be outside if you're carrying an emotional umbrella ready to pop over your head.

MY LEAST FAVOURITE COLOUR

How can we make sure we're carrying an imaginary brolly and wellies for the emotional storms that life will throw at us?

First, we need to take a few steps back and think about one important thing. What is most likely to make us angry, stressed or afraid in the first place? What fills the rain clouds of our mind with so many water droplets that a shower has to follow? What are the triggers that make us happy, sad, afraid or excited?

The causes of these feelings are often very individual. Orange might be *your* favourite colour, but at the age of nine or ten I was afraid just to look at it. Orange paint on the walls, an orange plastic chair in a classroom or an orange-coloured shopping bag were all enough to send me running from the room. It always felt bigger than me, as if an orange curtain had wrapped itself around me and I could no longer see. In fact, one time a bully at school actually did wrap me up in an orange curtain, making me feel so sick that I felt like I was about to burst. (We'll cover bullying in more detail in chapter 3.)

Today I've made my peace with orange, but there are still things that can trigger a meltdown in me. I get anxious in large crowds or busy places. Loud, sudden noises like ambulance sirens make me want to run away. And I absolutely **HATE** the noise of leaf blowers in people's gardens.

To you, these might sound like silly things to be afraid of, but for me they are very real. That's me, but we're all different, and one person's favourite thing might be another's worst nightmare. The things that make us stressed or anxious are always personal, and no one else can ever say how big or how small something should feel to you. That's your decision. A big part of learning to manage our emotions is knowing what our personal trigger points are and being more aware of them. If we know that we are going to find something stressful or difficult, then we can take it more slowly, ask for help or try and break it down into smaller steps that will be easier to manage.

Whereas if we get caught *unaware*, then the warning lights that start flashing in our brain will be very real, and so will the fear, excitement or anger that we feel as a result. It's like being caught in that very sudden, very heavy rain shower. This is what releases adrenaline through the body and pushes us into 'fight or flight' mode.

The things that make us STRESSED or EXCITED, which push us into 'FIGHT OR FLIGHT' mode, are individual. And so are our ways of coping with them.

Like lots of autistic people, I do something called **STIMMING** (self-stimulating behaviour) to keep myself on an even keel: things that I can do on repeat, **AGAIN** and **AGAIN**, which create a comforting sense of rhythm. I used to make weird, unrelated movements when I felt something intensely, to help me communicate it to myself. You may laugh now, but I just recently found out that this is actually a very well-known method in acting that helps train famous actors for their roles in films. Watch out, Zendaya!

Rocking backward and forward on a chair, saying the same phrase over and over, or fidgeting with a toy are all things I have done to feel calm in stressful situations (even though they can make other people uncomfortable because they look odd). At moments where I've wanted to flee the room, scared of things other people haven't even noticed, these routines have helped me to focus and feel calm.

This was **HARD** at school, when the bright lights and loud bell would set off fireworks all over my body. But I learned that you need to experiment, find what works for you and get teachers to help you make the environment safe and comfortable. In particular, I found it helpful to have a routine around stressful parts of the day like leaving the house, arriving at school and going to bed. Having the comfort of a particular toy, a piece of music or a parent's hand to hold at the right time can make such a big difference.

Even I will admit that some of the things I have done to manage my emotions are pretty strange. Sometimes after school I would spend hours pushing a wheelbarrow along the drive outside my house, because I liked the solid feeling of controlled movement and the sound of it crunching through the gravel. More recently, I've discovered that I am comforted by the

sensation of curling my hair through my fingers, or by eating the same thing for lunch every day. The familiar way these things feel and taste help me to feel safe in anxious moments. They ground me to a point where everything feels in balance again.

Now, this all might sound very odd to you, but we are all **DIFFERENT**. We all find quiet and calm in our own way.

But perhaps you're not sure what your emotional 'umbrella' is or should be. How do you start trying to find it?

Like a true scientist, **EXPERIMENT**! Try different things when you sense the clouds coming and feel yourself going into 'fight or flight' mode. Keep a journal of what you did and how it made you feel. That's what I did, and it's what led to me writing this book. Over time, you can start to make a list of the things that work in different situations: your own personal survival guide for all weathers.

Most importantly, remember we won't always be able to stop ourselves from letting emotions get the better of us. Adults cry too and that is completely fine, because sometimes what we all need is a good sob, embracing our emotions so we can process the sadness,

anxiety or overwhelming happiness we are feeling. Much like farts, they are better out than in!

This isn't about stopping the emotional storms that define our lives, because we can't and we shouldn't want to. But we do have to be able to deal with them, to manage them so that we stay in the driver's seat of our mind and body.

And the key to that is teaching ourselves to see them coming. Just like we know there is probably rain around the corner when the sky is darkening and the air starts to feel heavy, we can sometimes sense situations where we are starting to get tense and unhappy, when continuing in the same direction is going to lead to some kind of meltdown. And that's when we need to step away, count to ten and reach for the biggest and brightest umbrella we can find: one that makes us feel safe, seen and heard.

The more we live in different weathers, the better we become at coping with them. And come rain or shine, we all have the capacity (and the need) to laugh, cry, hug and smile: to experience our biggest emotions without becoming the prisoner of them.

Bring on the umbrellas and sunglasses. **I always make sure to pack both.**

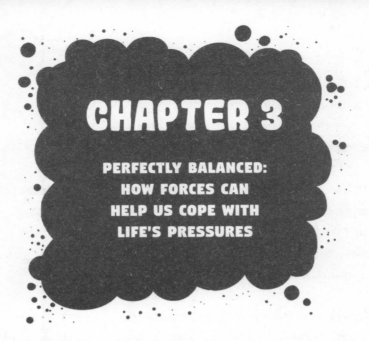

CHAPTER 3

PERFECTLY BALANCED: HOW FORCES CAN HELP US COPE WITH LIFE'S PRESSURES

When I was in primary school, every day would begin outside, with all of us standing in long lines in the playground while our teachers took the register.

It might sound strange, but often this was the most difficult part of the day for me. I hated having to stand still without fidgeting. My mind, which enjoys routine, didn't like the way the lines formed in a new order every morning – with different people ahead, behind and either side of me.

Also, it was usually too cold!

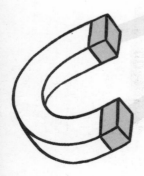

As I stood in that line, two competing thoughts were pulling me in different directions. One was compelling me to do what I was told: to stand still like everyone else and wait for my name to be taken. And there was another feeling, coming from within, that told me this was stupid, which made me start to panic, and gave me the strong desire to run away very fast.

Often, the second of these feelings would win the tug-of-war. My head would start to twitch, my arms would windmill and often I would run away crying.

It was just too hard having to think constantly about standing still, the unequal lines either side of me and the strangeness of conducting this daily ritual out in the cold instead of in our warm classroom.

What I realise now is that those feelings, that daily battle in my head and body, map closely on to one of the most important ideas in science – **FORCES**.

A force is something applied to an object as a push or pull. And these forces hold our whole world together.

GRAVITY is a force, keeping our feet (and everything else) on the ground. Pushing the brakes on your bike creates a force (known as friction), slowing you down when needed. The fish fingers you might eat for lunch

exert a downward force on your
plate, which pushes back with a
force of equal strength – keeping
everything in place. (At least until you start eating them.)

If we want to understand our world and why things
move, speed up, slow down, stay together, fall apart
or just stand still, then we *need* to understand forces.
They are the silent and unseen masters of everything
around us.

Even better, they are a great way of thinking about our
own lives.

Because we all face forces that may not exist according
to the physics textbook, but which constantly push and

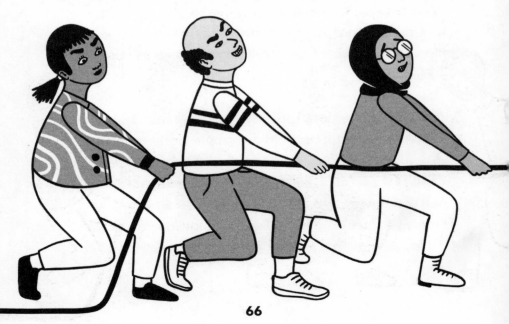

pull us in different directions – like peer pressure, other people's expectations and our own wants and fears.

Standing in the registration line each morning, I felt the tug of *these* forces on me: emotions that felt every bit as strong as gravity and friction.

There was the force of what my body and mind wanted: to escape and run away. There was the force of what other people expected of me: to stand quietly in line and wait for my name to be taken. And there was the force that comes from worrying about what other people will say or think – wanting to do the same as everyone else so that I wouldn't stick out or be laughed at (we call this one **PEER PRESSURE**). As I've described, every morning at school was a battle between these forces, and I didn't always know which one was going to win.

But it got a lot easier for me to understand what was going on after I learned about physical forces and how important they are.

I think you'll find the same. So let's explore the world of forces, and then let's think about what it means for our own worlds.

THE HIDDEN WIZARDS OF THE WORLD

Forces are invisible, and unfortunately even the most advanced scientific equipment won't allow you to see them.

But although we can't see forces work, we can witness the *results* of those forces all around us.

On a busy road, every bike, bus and car is being moved (and stopped) by forces. Switch on a light, and the electricity that makes it work is powered by forces. Stick a magnet on the fridge, and you're watching a force (magnetism) at work. In fact, just being alive is the product of all sorts of forces inside your body (a bit complicated, but I will explain).

Forces are great because: 1. they are everywhere, and 2. they explain so much.

There are many different types of forces, and there are various scientific ways of categorising them. To make things easy, I want to show you just two ways of thinking about forces: **CONTACT FORCES** and **NON-CONTACT FORCES**.

The difference between these is whether objects have to actually collide – to come into contact with each other – for a force to happen between them.

A good example of a contact force is **FRICTION**: the force experienced when an object passes through or along another. We all know what friction is because we experience it every time our feet hit the floor when we are walking or running.

And we *need* friction because it's one of the things that allows us to slow down (and to get a grip – ha!). Without friction we would be falling over a lot and cars wouldn't be able to brake so quickly. If you've ever slipped when walking on an icy pavement, then you have an idea of what a world with much less friction would look like.

But friction doesn't just happen when two solid objects collide. It also occurs when objects pass through the air or water. The friction makes it harder for the object to move, slowing it down, a bit like how we all feel on a day when things aren't going well.

For example, if you are playing a game of catch, the ball experiences a form of friction (called air resistance or drag) as it passes through the air after you have thrown it. This explains why the same throw would travel further at the top of a mountain than in your school playground: when we are higher up ('at altitude'), there are literally fewer gas molecules in the air, meaning there is also less friction to slow down your throw.

For another example of how air resistance works, look at skydiving – a sport where people jump out of planes in mid-air and then open a parachute to help bring them safely back to earth. It's the large surface area of the billowy parachute that increases air resistance, slowing down the diver's descent enough to reduce the force when they hit the ground to a safe level. **PHEW!**

That's friction: a contact force that slows us down, often when we need it most.

It's also a force that has been essential to human life and survival for our entire existence. Think of what happens when you rub your hands quickly together on a cold day: they will soon start to feel hot, the result of the kinetic energy (movement) being transferred into heat energy. Do the same with some dry sticks and you create not just heat but **FIRE**, because the wood gets so hot it produces sparks, which create a flame.

So friction has been pretty important in the history of humanity, as it continues to be today.

But not all forces rely on objects colliding with each other. Welcome to the equally important world of non-contact forces.

DROP IT!

The most familiar of these non-contact forces is gravity, the one that keeps us on the ground. This is the 'pull' made by the earth on all the objects in what is known as its gravitational field. It was most famously proved by the scientist Isaac Newton, who was inspired when he saw an apple fall out of a tree. Some say it landed on his head!

For another example, think back to our skydiver. When they jump out of the plane, it's gravity that is pulling them back down to earth.

GRAVITY has always been a force close to my heart. When I was feeling at my most anxious growing up, I would ask to be wrapped up tightly in a heavy blanket. The force it exerted on me – its gravity – helped to keep me still and slowly allowed me to feel safe and calm again.

Alongside gravity, one of the most important non-contact forces is *electrostatic*. You might not have heard of this one before, but this is the force that happens between objects that carry a positive and negative charge. Let me explain ...

Every atom (the tiny building blocks that *all* things are made of) contains both positively charged *protons* and negatively charged *electrons*. Protons live in the middle of the atom (called the nucleus), and electrons float around on the outer layer.

It is the behaviour of electrons that starts to make things interesting. Because they are both lighter and nearer to the surface of the atom, they react easily when they come into contact with other atoms. An atom can lose electrons, at which point it becomes positively charged; or it can gain them and become negatively charged.

This is why your hair sticks up when you rub a balloon over it (an experiment you have probably done in science lessons).

The friction of rubbing transfers electrons from your hair to the balloon, which becomes *negatively* charged (–) as a result, and your lovely locks become *positively* charged (+).

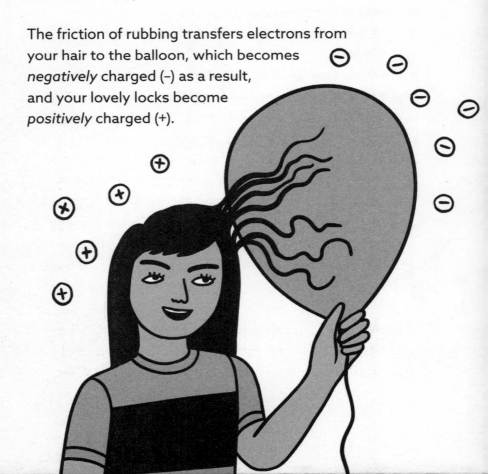

When atoms become 'charged' in this way, either by losing or gaining electrons, a force starts to happen between them: **ELECTROSTATIC FORCE**. This causes similarly charged atoms (+ and + or - and -) to *repel* each other and oppositely charged ones (+ and -) to *attract* each other.

A positively charged atom will attract a negatively charged one but push away another positive. Similarly, two negatives will run away from each other.

This is why your hair sticks up in the experiment. You've generated opposite charges on the atoms in your hair and on the surface of the balloon. These **ATTRACT** each other, making the hair stick to the balloon as you move it away from your head.

This electrostatic force is something that we rely on to live and function. Our bodies use it to transmit messages from one place to another, making sure everything keeps working. We depend on this flow of positive and negative charges to tell different parts of the body to repair themselves, feel pain, start digesting the food we have eaten or respond to a threat such as infection.

By now, you are hopefully starting to realise quite how important forces are to pretty much every aspect of our world! We might not be able to see these hidden levers of our universe, but by understanding them we can start to illuminate the visible world that surrounds us every day.

PHYSICAL FORCES, HUMAN FEELINGS

But what do scientific forces have to tell us about the pressures we feel in our own lives? Well, if you start to think about your life – at home, at school, with friends – then it's easy to see that you are subject to many invisible pushes and pulls that act just like the forces we have already explored.

Here are some examples of these forces – ones that don't exist in the same way as gravity or friction, but which we *feel* just as much as if they were real.

- There are things we are attracted to or repulsed by just like electrically charged particles. We might **LOVE** a swimming lesson so much that we rush to get ready for it, or **DISLIKE** getting in the water so much that we do everything possible to put it off (think about how people who dislike swimming actually seem to recoil from getting in the water, as if they share an electrical charge with it and are being pushed away from the pool).

76

There are things that feel like such a **NATURAL** and **IMPORTANT** part of our world that we can't imagine life without them – like our parents, brothers and sisters, best friends or favourite toys. These are like our **GRAVITY**: they keep us grounded and make us feel safe when we are pulled towards them.

There are pressures we face, as if we were a table on which a very heavy book has just been placed, exerting a force downwards that requires us to push back just as hard – because the laws of physics tell us that every action creates an equal and opposite reaction. That might be peer pressure, the feeling that you have to do or say things because other people are trying to make you do them. It might be the pressure of an upcoming event you want to do well in, like an exam or a match. Or it might be, like I often experienced, the pressure of feeling you are meant to fit in when you know that your brain and body just work differently. We call this the **INNER CRITIC**: a silent voice that magnifies every doubt in our mind and makes every bad report or negative comment we have ever received feel like it is blaring through a loudspeaker.

⚛️ Alongside these 'downward' pressures, we encounter a sort of friction in our lives. Maybe we have to finish homework before we are allowed to watch TV, or save up pocket money before being able to buy that new pair of trainers, or miss out on something we enjoy as a punishment. Just like in the real world, these frictions may slow us down, but they can also be what we need, giving us a natural pause that's good for helping us think (even if it doesn't feel like it at the time).

⚛️ Finally, just like in the world around us, emotional forces sometimes compete. Like when the gravity pulling a skydiver down to earth is countered by the action of the parachute generating air resistance. Similarly, we may find ourselves in situations where we feel we are being pulled in different directions at the same time, like I used to be when standing in the registration line each morning.

These emotional 'forces' surround our lives just as much as gravity and electricity control our bodies. And, just like with forces in physics, we are better equipped to handle them if we understand them properly. So let's finish by looking at how we can think about, and deal with, these forces.

GRAB A PEN AND PAPER, OR YOUR PHONE, AND WRITE DOWN ONE 'POSITIVE' FORCE IN YOUR LIFE AND ONE 'NEGATIVE' ONE. NOW THINK ABOUT THEM AS YOU READ ON.

HOW TO THINK YOUR FEELINGS

Recognising the existence of these emotional 'forces' can be a massive help when dealing with some of life's more difficult situations.

Often, when we feel bad, it is because some kind of force is being exerted on us, by either ourselves or other people.

We might be **AFRAID** of something that we have to do today, like that dreaded swimming lesson.

We might be about to do something that we know is

going to be **DIFFICULT**, with lots of friction involved –
like a long run, or a tough piece of homework.

Or we might feel that people are trying to **FORCE** us into
doing something. Like peer pressure, when someone
tells you to do or say something 'because everyone else
is'. Or bullying, when someone is actually trying to make
you feel bad.

So it's helpful to be able to recognise the difference
between these types of forces so we can decide how
best to respond.

It might be about doing something you don't like
because it's actually good for you: like if a parent asks
you to eat your vegetables or revise for a spelling test.
The force here is a concerned parent who wants the best
for you and knows that sometimes you will benefit from
doing things you don't enjoy.

Or it might be about *not* doing something because you
realise that the force at work is bullying or peer pressure,
where your needs and feelings aren't considered. Like
the time when a girl at school tried to persuade me to
take off my skirt and run around the playground during
lunch break.

She was trying to bully me, to humiliate me by making

other people laugh at me for doing something weird and revealing. Thinking about this situation through the lens of forces helped me to see what was really going on. Running around without my skirt on wasn't going to be 'cool' or 'funny' like this girl said. It was just going to be embarrassing for me, and a way for her to feel powerful.

Whatever the difficult situation might be, if you think about it hard enough you can usually recognise a force at work, and the person or people exerting it.

Maybe someone else is trying to **HELP** and **SUPPORT** you.

Maybe they are trying to **BULLY** or put pressure on you. (See the box at the end of this chapter for more on bullying.)

Maybe you are putting pressure on **YOURSELF** (like worrying too much about a test that is important, but not *that* important).

You might find your own unique way of articulating the pressures that you feel. I used to tap my arms to mimic and visualise the things I sensed and felt around me. To me this felt more 'real' than a feeling in my head: it stimulated another sense and allowed me to both understand better and think more clearly.

Even today I will sometimes 'tap out' an important decision to give myself a sense of reassurance, as often in autism we can feel the pressure but not know what it is. This is very common in autism, where it is hard to identify what you feel, and so to make it real and visible you find a language to make it seen or heard. Weighted blankets were really useful in calming me down as they put equal pressure on my body that made me feel hugged, slowing me down so I could process.

The important thing is to recognise the human and emotional forces that exist in your life and work out how you can respond to them in the **BEST WAY**.

This can help you realise that these forces are often a good and **IMPORTANT** thing. We need friction in our lives, just as surely as we need it from our shoes. We need sources of dependable gravity. And we can't escape the electric force of peer pressure, though we can decide how we will respond to it.

Once we recognise these forces, we can see peer pressure for what it is and filter the people who actually like us from those who are trying to get us to do something for them. We can listen to our inner critic in a way that doesn't allow it to drown out all other thoughts. And we can think about the critical things people say about us in a new light.

Maybe the criticism was coming from a teacher who wanted to help us, and is worth taking seriously.
Or perhaps it was just a nasty comment from someone in your class who was *feeling pressure of their own*, and so shouldn't be taken seriously – because what they said tells us more about them than it does us and how they are in turn are affected by the forces in their life.

If we only *feel* the forces that surround us then it is easy to get overwhelmed by them: to allow fear about next week's exam to grow in your belly like a weed, or to let someone's nasty words rub off on you like wet paint. But if we start to *think* about these forces, to recognise and understand them, then the power is in our hands.

Think back to our skydiver. They need the parachute to provide air resistance and reduce the gravitational force that is pulling them towards the ground. We can do something similar when we encounter problems: the ability to pause and slow down, to think our feelings and work out what forces are pushing or pulling us, is a parachute that we can use every day of our lives.

Bullying is an unpleasant part of growing up that most of us will see happening at school, even if we aren't the direct target of it.

In simple terms, a bully is someone who tries to make another person feel scared, upset or embarrassed about themselves. They will do this either through physical attacks (even small ones, like shoving or pinching), threats of what they might do (like hurting you or spreading untrue rumours about you), or through verbal attacks in which they constantly criticise or taunt you and try to get other people to do the same.

Bullying might happen out in the playground in plain view, or it could be done silently and unseen to the rest of the world through messages on your phone.

Whatever way a bully chooses to operate, they usually have the same motivation: the same force pushing on them. They want to feel powerful. This is why they make threats and try to make you do things for them.

Bullying can be hard to deal with, whether it is happening to you or to someone you know. But there are a few things to know about it, and a few more that you can do if you see it happening.

Some things to know:

- Bullies, who often seem so scary, are usually *afraid of something themselves*. They are behaving the way they do because they want to *feel* a power, control and confidence in their lives that they don't *actually* have. For example, if a bully is being nasty to you about having 'no friends', it probably means they feel insecure about their own popularity.

- Generally speaking, people who are happy and confident in themselves don't become bullies. It is people who are trying to deal with problems of their own who do. They may present as being powerful and successful, but they are almost certainly not. They are trying to exert the force of bullying on you because *they* are under pressure from their own forces: feeling worried about whatever is going on in their life. You are the victim of this bullying, but you are *not* the problem or the cause. It is not your fault.

Some things to do:

- Find someone to **TALK** to and get **HELP**. Bullies will try and stop you from doing this. They might promise to make your life even harder if anyone finds out. Ignore this, because a large part of the bully's power is keeping you silent, so that no one can help and they hold all the power. Once their mum finds out what they have been doing and how they have been treating other people, that power will often quickly drain away like water down the plughole.

- It can be really hard to admit that horrible things have been happening to you. But in **99%** of cases, telling a parent or friend what has been happening will be the most important step towards getting the problem solved.

- At the same time, parents and teachers won't always be there for us when the bullying is actually happening. The best advice here is also the hardest to follow: don't rise to the bait, get angry or lash out at the bully. They get satisfaction from watching you become upset or do something that means they can pretend you were actually the one causing problems. In the moment, the best response is to do and say nothing. Show that you are the **BIGGER PERSON** and ignore them. Then, if they don't get bored and the bullying continues, get help from a responsible adult to sort it out properly.

CHAPTER 4

PERFECTLY ALIVE:
FIND YOUR PASSIONS
WITH PHOTOSYNTHESIS

What's the coolest thing you have ever done in a classroom? Mine was in an English lesson during Year 9 when I presented my own **LANGUAGE**: a special code that only I knew how to speak and translate. It was made up of weird words, taps on the body and beeping noises like a computer might make. It was called Epas (after two conditions I knew well and which made me different: epilepsy and autism spectrum disorder).

My presentation was met with a slightly confused silence, but I felt thrilled to be sharing my secret with the world. This language was important to me. I had spent years organising the unique way in which I communicated through words and gestures that many

POP!

PARP

people found strange, but which I needed to process the ideas and feelings that were buzzing around my head.

Squeaks, jerky movements and little sprints would **BURST** out of me like a musical instrument (including my favourite noise: **'PARP'!**).

This would happen (and still does) when I felt stressed, like a bulging suitcase that will burst open if it's not unpacked. The noises and gestures were how I expressed myself as someone who struggled with 'normal' human ways of communicating.

ZONK

I also found other ways to express myself, including through music. I often played guitar in a band, which allowed me to be among other people without having to say a thing. I could let my performance speak all the thoughts and feelings that I wasn't able to put into words.

It was the same with my piano at home, where I play 'by ear' (not from written music but by copying tunes I hear). Learning to play a new melody well was just as fun and exciting as a fresh science experiment. It took me away from the things I thought or worried about most of the time. With my fingers running across the piano keys and the soothing notes twisting around the room, I sometimes felt like I wasn't sitting down at all. I was floating.

ping

twang

BANG

Writing was similar. Every afternoon I would sit down with my diary to write, doodle and draw what had happened that day. Often, what I produced wouldn't make sense to anyone else, but it gave me a precious sense of **PEACE** and solace. It was my world: one I owned and only I could understand, which I would go back to every day just for the love of it.

Music and writing weren't just different ways of expressing myself in a confusing world. They were also two of the things I most enjoyed doing in the world. And they still are.

In other words, they were my **PASSIONS**. The things that made me jump out of bed in the morning, which I spent all day thinking about and which I always felt good doing. They made every day manageable.

Passions like these are important, because there is a difference between the things we depend on to live and those we need to really be *alive*.

We all need food to eat, a home to live in and enough sleep every night. These are the things that keep our bodies and minds ticking over. They are life's essentials – like flour in a cake or violins in an orchestra.

squeak

But being able to eat, sleep and stay safe are not *everything* that we require to live our lives. We also need family and friends who care about us, and we them. We need the fuel to pursue ambitions that require lots of work and practice to achieve. And we need *passions* that get us excited every time we are doing them.

Science was my way to understand the world – my bread and butter. But music, drawing and writing were my passions: outlets for my energy that relaxed and decompressed me like a whoopee cushion, so I could feel normal again (well, my perfectly weird normal).

Your passions might be a sport you love to watch and play, the kind of books you most like to read, or trying new recipes in the kitchen. You might enjoy building things, crafting, dancing or swimming, or the act of helping people and making them feel good.

The important thing is not what your passions are, but to know that you have them. Caring about something, in a way that makes you think about it every day and constantly search out new things to watch or read about it, is the telltale sign that you have a passion brewing deep inside.

And if you want to know why that matters, then take a walk with me in this chapter around your favourite park or garden. The trees and flowers are going to tell us everything we need to know about why passions are such an essential part of life.

HELLO, SUN

Think about any tree, plant or flower. What does it need to survive?

It needs to be planted in the ground or in some soil so it can grow roots that suck up water from below the surface (where it collects when it rains).

It needs air, from which it can extract the gas carbon dioxide.

And it needs sunlight, the ingredient that makes it all happen.

It needs these three things to feed itself, through a process known as **PHOTOSYNTHESIS** – a plant's ability to make its own food.

This has been going on for a while – in fact, since 3.4 billion years ago (which is a very, very, very, very, **VERY** long time), when the first microorganism (extremely small living thing) converted sunlight into usable energy. Although it didn't know it at the time, it lit the spark for the rest of biology, a flame that continues to burn brightly today.

So what is photosynthesis and how does it work?

This might be something you have already learned at school or it might be completely new to you. But in simple terms, it is the very clever process by which plants use sunlight, water and carbon dioxide to make their own food (glucose), giving them the energy they need to grow. By doing this, they also create oxygen, which is released back into the atmosphere.

That's good news for us, because *we* need **OXYGEN**! We use it to unlock energy from the food we eat, via the chemical reaction of respiration. This happens when we breathe.

In fact, plants – especially ocean plants – are the **SINGLE BIGGEST** source of oxygen in the air that we humans (and other animals) breathe. So photosynthesis isn't just plants keeping themselves alive. It's also doing the same for every animal on the planet, **YOU** included!

As we humans breathe in oxygen and expel carbon dioxide, plants everywhere do the exact opposite. They use the carbon dioxide and produce more oxygen for us to breathe. This is the cycle that keeps animal and plant life going.

Clearly plants are extremely clever and useful organisms: capable of not only feeding themselves but also supporting a large part of life on Earth. So remember to give the next tree you meet a pat on the back (and feel free to name it if you like, just for fun. I'll start ... how about Dave or Mandy?).

There are three key ingredients in making photosynthesis happen. I want to focus on just one of them, because I think it can tell us something about how we live and grow as people.

I want to talk about **SUNLIGHT**.

Because while water and carbon dioxide may be key ingredients for the marvel that is photosynthesis, sunlight is its secret sauce.

It is sunlight that makes **EVERYTHING** happen.
It provides the energy for the reaction – just like you
need a hot oven or hob to cook food. It excites a
chemical in the leaves called chlorophyll, enabling the
plant to harness the energy to turn carbon dioxide and
water into precious glucose.

A plant absorbs sunlight through its leaves, which are
often large and flat to suck up as much of that delicious
light as possible. I love this about plants – how they are
designed by nature to capture light with every bit of
every leaf, as if stretching out and wrapping round to
give the sun a big hug.

This is why you will often see plants growing at strange
angles or in one particular direction. This is not for
fun, but so that they can be as close as possible to the
source of sunlight and not block one another (which is
cute). If you put a potted plant on your kitchen counter
away from the nearest window, watch how its stem and
leaves will grow over time towards that window, helping
it to absorb as much sunlight as possible to power
photosynthesis.

I think that's similar to the role that passions play in our
lives as humans. It's our passions that provide us with
energy. They get us running to put on our football kit,
to try out a new cake recipe or to get hold of a new

book from our favourite writer. Just like the plant growing towards the sunny window, we are motivated by the things we care about and are interested in. We gravitate **TOWARDS** them. They are our sunlight.

And just like sunlight alters the shape of the plant, we are changed by the things we love to do. Building models or LEGO teaches us the patience needed to create something of our own. Playing lots of sport or learning a musical instrument shows us how much we need to practise something to get better at it. Reading lots of books helps us to see the world in a different way, and to understand how others see it.

Passions can give us **ENERGY**, as we get excited about doing them, but they also require us to put the energy and effort *in*: watering the soil to help them grow and grow.

If we do this, our passions can become so much more than things we enjoy doing. They grow into a part of us – something we can't imagine our lives without.

DIGGING FOR GOLD

Our passions matter. We can probably all agree about that. But that doesn't mean they are **EASY**.

Passions often energise and excite you. But they can also come from feelings of injustice, frustration or anger – a desire to act without always knowing how. In 2018, a schoolgirl called Greta Thunberg was so anxious to get politicians to do more about the climate crisis that she spent weeks doing a sit-down protest outside the parliament in Sweden, her home country. What began with just one person quickly grew into a global movement, making Greta one of the most influential voices in the world on the need for climate action.

Not all our passions may have such a big global impact (!), but we can still learn from Greta,

96

especially about how what starts small can grow big with the right attention.

A passion needs space to **GROW** and an environment it can grow into. It needs to be 'watered' with the care and attention that we dedicate to it. Just like how a plant will wither without being properly looked after, we will also suffer if we don't nurture our passions by giving them the time and space they deserve. If we don't do that, an important part of us becomes neglected, which can mean bad moods and worse as a result.

A passion is not a hobby, although one can grow into another over time.

Hobbies are things we enjoy and like to do, but we might not miss them too much if they were taken away from us. Passions go **DEEPER**. They are things we do because we love and care about them. They are almost a part of us, something we can't imagine ourselves without.

That isn't to say that hobbies are a bad thing. Trying things and working out that we don't particularly like them, or that we like doing something else better, is all part of growing up. We won't all be avid readers, natural goal scorers or brilliant bakers. There were subjects I really didn't like at school, such as history, and things that never interested me, like painting my nails.

But that's fine. We can't love or enjoy everything in life. And once you find something that you are really interested in, a source of sunlight that you just *have* to move towards, then you are much more likely to push the 'go' button and put the effort in.

Finding those passions – or letting them find us – is a **BIG** part of the puzzle.

But we also have to learn to hold on to them. Which can be harder than it sounds, thanks to our old friend from the last chapter, peer pressure.

Maybe someone at school tells you it isn't cool any more to have a poster of a particular band up on your wall. Maybe they try to tell you that maths is *boring*, reading is *sad* or your love for science fiction is *weird*.

Maybe it isn't just one person. Maybe almost everyone in your class shares the same view. Maybe you're only one of two or three people you know who like playing this game or listening to that music.

What do you do then? Do you stop doing something you **LOVE** because someone else told you that it shouldn't be fun, interesting or cool?

Many of us hide our passions because we are embarrassed. We tell ourselves 'I can't be bothered', when we really mean 'I'm worried what other people think about this'.

I hope that you don't do this. I hope that the voice you listen to is the one inside you, telling you what it is you really enjoy and want to do.

This is a path we all have to **LEARN** to walk in our own way, because it isn't easy going against the crowd (and you won't always have to). But one thing I learned is that there is nothing worse than trying to *fake* a passion.

Pretending you care about something to impress a friend or classmate might seem like a good idea, but it can leave you feeling empty (and tired from having to act) – exactly the opposite of the excitement and energy we feel when we are doing something we really love. It is like a plastic plant: one that won't grow however much you water it and shower it in sunlight.

When I was at school, there were several times I decided that the way to become happy and popular was to imitate what the other girls around me did. I tried wearing the same clothes as them, watching the same TV shows and talking the same way they did, which I often found boring.

None of this made me feel good. In fact, it had the opposite effect. Because I wasn't just doing things that I didn't really want to do. I was also missing out on the chance to spend that time on the things I did enjoy – like music, writing and science projects.

I learned my lesson and never tried to deny myself my real passions again.

There is one way we are *different* from our hero in this chapter – the photosynthesising plant. There is only one sun, and all plants grow towards it, trying to capture as much of its glow as they can.

But humans can have **MANY** passions, hobbies and things to love in life. We are all individuals with our own very **PERSONAL** interests. These don't have to 'make sense' according to normal stereotypes. We can be fanatical footballers at the same time as loving maths and science. We can be punk rock fans who also enjoy baking cupcakes. There is no shame in what makes you tick: it's your own source of energy that is designed by and suited to you.

Whatever your passions may be, the most important thing is to be true to them. Don't look to anyone else for approval. Give yourself permission to pursue the passion that's in you. Move and grow towards your own source of sunlight.

CHAPTER 5

PERFECTLY AT HOME: DISCOVER YOUR NATURAL HABITAT

'Bring the fourth cushion, please, Mum!'

It was a conversation we had every bedtime until I was twelve, which followed a careful and important routine. An extra cushion would be brought into my bedroom, I would arrange all four in the shape of a T, then I'd carefully place my body over the vertical part and lay my head on the crossbar. My bunny rabbit toy would sit next to me. And only then, when my mum tucked me in tight like a sausage roll, when the light and the pressure of the duvet felt just right, was I able to fall asleep.

My bedroom cocoon was just one of several closely controlled environments that I relied on to feel safe and happy. At times, when my head would freeze with all the thoughts that seemed to be trying to burst out of it, I took refuge in a cardboard box. This feeling of being enclosed and isolated was what I needed to calm the waves that were crashing around inside me. It allowed me to feel like I was in **CONTROL**, in a place of my own where bad thoughts and overwhelming feelings couldn't hurt me.

I loved these moments of complete calm so much that I would try to hold on to them, blinking my eyes quickly ten times to 'save' my game so I could return to it when needed.

Not all of these safe places were confined spaces. I also loved being at the top of a hill, sitting with my rucksack, water and biscuits, looking out over the Welsh countryside and feeling that I had a place in this world. I loved the silent presence of the trees, the whistling of the wind and the sight of fields and hills rolling further than I could see. Together, these hugs of nature seemed to offer more acceptance than I often found from other people.

Even today, all grown up, I have places where I go to feel safe and to free myself from the thoughts or fears

bubbling up inside me. The cardboard box is long gone, but sometimes I will still sit under my desk when experiencing anxiety. Having that 'roof' over my head is usually enough to make me feel safer. It takes away the sharpest edges of an anxiety attack and allows me to think clearly again.

Most of all, when I am having a bad day, the place I really want to be is the science lab. Because when I am working on a difficult problem, wrestling with new information or trying to make sense of what I have found, there isn't space in my head for anything else. I find my work in science so completely absorbing that it crowds out all the big fears and bad thoughts that peck away at me. Science gives me the precious gift of being able to **FOCUS** – no longer distracted by the noise in my head, something strange I have seen or an unpleasant smell I have just noticed.

The first time I stepped foot in a science lab, I knew I had found my **NATURAL HABITAT**: the place I was born to be and where I felt most comfortable. In the lab, everything seems to fit: like a key in a lock, or your feet in your favourite pair of slippers. I always feel like I have come home.

A HOME WITHIN A HOME

We all have a 'home' like this: a habitat which is our perfect environment for life.

In fact, we have several.

The first and most important is the one we all share: planet Earth. As far as we know (unless you have any new information about alien landings, or have seen one from your bedroom window), this planet is the only place in the universe capable of supporting animal life.

Earth may be tiny as far as the universe is concerned, but it's also pretty neatly designed. It's close enough to the sun that we don't freeze to death, but not so close that temperatures get out of hand. Its atmosphere gives us oxygen to breathe and protects us from lots of the nasty stuff (poisonous gases and deadly radiation) floating around the solar system. It also provides some useful extras, like water to drink. A pretty good package all round!

So the planet is our shared home and the natural habitat for all human life. That's the first layer.

Within it we have our own homes: the places we live and the people we share them with – a habitat of family and friends, familiar spaces and comfy chairs where we feel 'at home'.

Then I would argue that there's a *third* layer, which is our habitat as an individual: the place or places where we feel like the best version of ourselves, most free and able to express our thoughts and feelings. Like my cardboard box, Welsh hillside or science lab.

These habitats are what I want to talk about in this chapter. Because, when we're growing up, they are the only ones we get to choose and make entirely our own. These are the worlds that we create and live in: the places where we feel most alive.

So let's talk more about how we can find and explore yours.

WHO'S GOT EIGHT EYES AND EIGHT LEGS?

As humans, we're far from alone in having a natural habitat in which we thrive.

In fact, every plant and animal you can possibly think of has their own habitat. And every bit of this remarkable planet we live on – from the hottest desert to the coldest

ice cap, the deepest ocean to the tallest rainforest –
provides a habitat for some kind of life. You might not
be able to live there, but what's too hot, cold, wet or dry
for us is perfect for something or someone else.

That means our world is full of weird and wonderful
living things that have adapted to live in some of the
strangest and most dangerous places on Earth.

- The Himalayan jumping spider has one of the
  highest homes on Earth – near the top of Mount
  Everest, where the food is so difficult to find that
  they have eight eyes to make sure
  they never miss a meal.

- And if you thought eight eyes was a bit much,
  what about another animal with eight legs?
  Allow me to introduce the *tardigrade* – a
  minuscule creature barely longer than a
  millimetre, which under a microscope looks
  a bit like a caterpillar. Its defining feature is its
  ability to expel almost all the water from
  its body and survive in a dehydrated
  state, neither breathing nor
  eating. This allows it to live almost
  anywhere on Earth – from the oceans
  to the jungle to the inside of volcanoes.
  They've even been taken to the moon!

✳ Now from one of the planet's smaller creatures to one of its largest. If you've ever seen a picture of a polar bear, perhaps you've wondered how these magnificent animals manage to survive the bitterly cold Arctic winters, when temperatures can be as low as -69°C (yes: 69 degrees *below freezing*). But they do survive, on average for between twenty-five and thirty of these winters, because of how cleverly they are adapted to this icy habitat. A polar bear's white fur helps it to blend in with their environment, while the black skin underneath is designed to soak up every bit of available heat from the sun. They grow fur all over – even on the pads of their paws, which also helps them to grip the slippery ice. And those paws are slightly webbed, helping them to swim around really efficiently from one sheet of ice to another.

Millions of species have adapted to live in many different habitats on Earth. We all live on the same planet – but our tiny piece of it is personal in all sorts of ways that might be dangerous, confusing or plain weird to a different species. An environment that would be deadly to one animal will be a comfy and familiar home to another.

As humans we already have our collective habitat. But as individuals that isn't enough. We also need to find our personal one: a habitat within a habitat – the special place in the world that is all our own.

BUILDING THE ECOSYSTEM

There are lots of different ways we can define our personal habitat as human beings.

It might be about a special **PLACE** or **SPACE**: your room, which you have organised and decorated in exactly the way you want.

It might be about **PEOPLE**: the ones who always make you feel at home, wherever you happen to be.

It might be about a **PASSION**: the thing you love to do and always feel best when you are doing it.

110

And it might be a bit of all those things together: the place you like to be, the thing you most enjoy doing and the people who you always want to share it with, all forming parts of what makes you happy.

Whatever it may be, you will know when you have found your habitat, because nothing else feels quite like it. When we are in these very personal places, nothing can touch us. We don't have to worry about what other people are thinking or what they might say. We don't wish we were somewhere else, with someone else, doing anything else. We are able just to live in the moment, being our true selves and not trying to hide or pretend anything.

It's a magical feeling of safety, comfort and happiness that we should all get to enjoy – **A LOT**!

So how do we find it?

You shouldn't expect it to magically appear overnight. It takes time to organise a room properly, to discover the things we really enjoy or to get to know people so that we feel really at home with them. Just like how a bird will spend around two weeks building a nest to lay eggs in, finding the right twigs to use and choosing the best place to arrange them.

It takes lots of small steps before the germ of something can grow into a full-blown personal habitat.

And to start walking those steps, you will need a map.

DRAW A MAP OF ALL THE MOST IMPORTANT PLACES IN YOUR UNIVERSE. WHY DO YOU LIKE THEM? WHEN DO YOU MOST LIKE TO GO TO THEM? WHO WOULD YOU CHOOSE TO BE IN THEM WITH YOU? AND MAYBE DRAW HOW THEY MAKE YOU FEEL, TOO.

Remember, when I say places, that could be literal: a physical space like your bedroom or the comfy chair at your nan's house. Or it could be a place you go in your head, like the feeling you get when you are reading your

favourite book or the thoughts you have when you're listening to a special piece of music.

All these places can be part of our habitat as people. And remember that the polar bear doesn't stay on one sheet of ice, but swims around all over the place, just as other animals roam right across the desert, rainforest or grassland that they call home. Our habitat might be made up of some specific *kinds* of places, but that doesn't mean we can't move around.

Nor does it mean our habitat won't change over time. As we grow up, meet new people and go into different environments (like a new school), we're going to want to add new things, change some of the furniture and switch around the posters on the wall. But the shape of that room probably doesn't change too much. If music is your passion now, it probably still will be in the future: you'll just like listening to different things. The 'places' we loved growing up are often the places we want to return to at all stages in life. They just might look a little different.

Having these places written down can remind us of where we like to go when we're happy, sad, anxious or in need of a hug – like a personal treasure map of our own lives, reminding us where all the emotional gold is buried.

And it's a **PERSONAL** map, because it won't mean much to someone else. The treasure it points to is yours: the places, people and things in your life to which you are as perfectly adapted as the Himalayan jumping spider is to life on Mount Everest.

Because you know the map better than anyone, it means you will always be able to get back to your natural habitat as quickly as you need to. This is an **IMPORTANT** thing to remember. Although as humans we share the same habitat on this earth, my personal habitat is different to yours, just as yours is different to your best friend's, and your brother's or sister's is different again. We are all the same species, but adapted in our own unique and special ways to a life that only we are going to live.

Now you might be asking yourself, if we all have these individual habitats, how do we all live together in families and friendships and relationships? That's a very good question – but life is all about compromise: making the most of the things we have in common at the same time as respecting the ones that make us different.

These compromises might mean we sometimes have to (or want to) travel out of our own habitat to spend time in someone's else's, because we love them. Maybe that means watching a game of football we're not interested in or trying a meal we might not choose for ourselves.

This makes the other person feel good about their choices and preferences: all the tiny but important things that make up *their* habitat. Learning to connect with others in this way, and being willing to go into unfamiliar territory, is all part of life's give and take. We can't spend our whole lives hanging out on our own little island, neither making trips nor welcoming guests. You would get very bored, not to mention hungry!

As we find this balance, we learn how much humans as a species rely on each other. We need other people, which means we need to respect and understand their habitats as well as our own.

My dad has a good description for this. He calls our family an 'ecosystem': a very lively jumble of lots of people with their own individual needs and personal preferences. This habitat of habitats is weird, lively and unpredictable, but it's also incredibly **PRECIOUS** because of that **DIVERSITY** and the fact that we really care for each other (just like the natural world is so beautiful because of its *biodiversity*: the huge range and variety of plant and animal life on Earth).

Maybe in theory this family ecosystem shouldn't work, but in reality it does. That's because we all know and nurture our own habitat, and we all respect each other's too. Even more importantly, it's because our parents had

the love to help us grow our own habitats at the cost of their own time, energy and sunlight. This is one of the **GREATEST** expressions of love any parent can give, and it's why working as a **TEAM** with your parents and those who love you is so important: because they really want the best for you and are willing to make sacrifices to help you achieve it. Remember that the next time they tell you to pick up your smelly socks!

Never forget that there are many more habitats than yours, and it's good to try visiting them sometimes. But before we can get comfortable elsewhere, we first need to find and define our own habitat.

Just like you wouldn't try to spend the Christmas holiday on an Arctic ice sheet, and the polar bear probably isn't going to spend Christmas Day unwrapping presents in your living room in front of the fire, everybody has to find and get comfy in the habitat that is made for them.

So get thinking, get drawing and start mapping. This is a **BEAUTIFUL** part of life. Because once you've created the map, you will always have the route back to a place of safety, comfort and happy memories. You'll always be able to find your way home.

CHAPTER 6

PERFECTLY DIGITAL: CAN COMPUTERS TEACH US HOW TO THINK?

Technology is often so **AMAZING** that exactly how it works it can be a bit of a mystery. Have you ever wondered how an iPad is able to follow your finger around the screen, how Alexa can actually hear and 'understand' what you say to it or how the controller in your hands is able to communicate with the screen in front of you – even with no wires involved? It's enough to make your brain hurt!

These were the kinds of questions I used to ask myself growing up, even though the technology of my childhood was a tad less advanced than it is now. Where you might click a few buttons to stream your favourite TV show or podcast, I had to put actual physical tapes into a special player (yes, really, ask your mum or dad).

Back then, I thought maybe there was some secret magic involved that I could take advantage of. Aged six, I took one of my dad's video tapes, with some boring old movie on it, and carefully rubbed out the name written in pencil on the label. In its place, I neatly wrote 'Barbie Castle' in my sparkly gel pen. And then I put the tape back in the player, crossing my fingers and shutting my eyes.

You're probably clever enough to realise that this didn't work. The same film started playing in front of me and Barbie was nowhere to be seen.

It was an early demonstration of how technology can sometimes disappoint or frustrate us. We'll run out of battery at the worst possible moment. We'll push a button that no longer does what it's meant to. Or the machine – be that a game, a search engine, or Alexa – won't understand what we want it to do.

I'm afraid this chapter is not going to explain or solve any of these problems. We won't be getting into the details of exactly how these machines work and why they break – that's complicated!

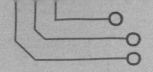

But I do want to look at one part of how computers work, which has an important lesson for us as humans. And that's the way they 'think' – or, in technical terms, how they process the information (aka data) they receive and use it to make decisions.

Because if you think about it, that is exactly what we are doing every single minute of our lives. We are constantly receiving information through all of our five senses, from how hot or cold a room is to whether the pavement feels slippery under our feet.

Then we are making decisions, like whether to put a jumper on or how quickly we can walk down the street without falling over.

Some of these decisions are easy: we make them without even having to think about it. If you've touched something that's too hot to handle, you will immediately yank your hand away because you feel pain. You don't spend ten seconds realising that you've burned your hand and deciding what to do next.

But other decisions *aren't* easy. The information is complicated and the answer isn't obvious. We actually have to think about it.

An example might be if you realise that a friend is sad about something, but don't know how best to help or comfort them. Should you try and talk to them about what's bothering them, or would they prefer not to discuss it?

In these situations, we will often spend ages thinking about what to do. We will agonise over which option to pick and question our judgement. We will probably lack **CONFIDENCE** in our ability to work out the 'right' thing to do.

Because we are human beings and not machines, emotions play a big part in these decisions. What we **DO** is often a result of how we **FEEL**. Which can be a problem. Sometimes our bad decisions (and we all make lots of them!) are a result of strong emotions. We do things we regret because we are tired, hungry or angry, and not thinking as clearly as we might otherwise be.

This is where computers have an advantage. Although they can't 'think' in the same creative way as you, they don't have these human feelings to trip them up. They just process the information and spit out the answer, or decision, that they have been programmed to find. They don't spend hours thinking about what to do or having a crisis of confidence about what they have decided.

Sounds easy? Well, let's take a closer look at how they do it and see if there's anything the computer can teach us about how to think more clearly and feel confident in our decisions.

THE SCIENCE OF (GOOGLE) SEARCH

Let's start with an example that will be familiar to everyone: the Google search. We all take for granted that by typing a few words into a search engine we can access information about absolutely anything in the world: stuff that would have taken hours of research in a library before the Internet existed.

But how does this incredibly helpful homework hack actually work?

Without getting into too much detail, there are two important parts to it. The first is what's known as indexing, which is the fancy word for creating a massive digital library of all the useful pages on the Internet, which Google does using a computer program called a spider (which works by 'crawling' the web. Very Halloween-y).

And when I say the digital library is massive, I mean **MASSIVE**: it contains hundreds of billions of web pages, which is itself just a fraction of all those that exist.

Then, when you type something into the search box, another bit of computer programming kicks in, known as ranking. This is the search engine's way of trying to work out what is going to be most relevant and important to you (for example, based on where in the world you are searching from and what you have searched for before).

So if I search for 'poodle' on Google (because I own a beautiful one called Wendy), my first page of results is going to be information about the dog breed from trusted sources. I'll also be prompted to search for other things specific to me: like where I can buy a poodle in the UK, how to find my local vet or where to buy dog toys. And if there have been recent news articles about poodles, I'll be shown those too.

In other words, behind every Google search there is a powerful computer program acting like a filter for the entire Internet, sifting out all the weird and unhelpful stuff to give you the results you are most likely to find useful. As a dog owner in England, I probably don't need to be told where a brilliant place for doggy day care in New York might be. (Although I might if I travelled there, and if I did the search engine would know about it ... spooky!)

Now let's take a step back for a moment. This ranking *algorithm* (a kind of computer program that provides a set of instructions for it to work with) may be incredibly clever and complex, but it also has a very simple idea behind it. It **ASKS QUESTIONS**. Is this page relevant? Is it up to date? Is it trustworthy? And many more – several hundred factors are considered in all.

But remember, not everything about these search engines is great. Just because a link is popular (something the ranking algorithm likes), it doesn't mean the information contained on the page is going to be useful or accurate. Don't believe everything you read online, including Wikipedia!

But there is one incredibly important thing that Google demonstrates: the importance of asking good questions and of questioning the information in front of you.

We can all learn from that. Because the more we ask, and the more closely we question something, the smarter we get. We can't think properly about things, or make good decisions, unless we have asked the right questions first and got our hands on (and wrapped our brains around) the most important information.

This is the very basis, the nuts and bolts, of science.

So let's start asking.

QUESTIONS, QUESTIONS ??

Ever since I can remember, I have always loved asking questions. I was always *that* kid in class putting their hand up, wanting to know a bit more than we were being taught. Like the scientist I would become, I was always trying to discover new things and work out if what I was being told was really true.

Of course, all children ask questions, especially when they are small and finding out about literally everything in the world around them. But here's the kicker: the older we get, the harder this can be. We can get stuck in our ways, like having our feet in wet mud. The more mature we become and the better we get at processing information, the less willing we often are to ask for it. (We call that a **PARADOX**: something that is true even though it doesn't seem to make sense.)

There's a reason for this – in fact, probably several. The person who puts up their hand to ask a question is going to be observed by everyone else in the class. If it's a 'silly' question, or one that they maybe should have known the answer to, then people might laugh at them.

In other words, before we ever ask a question in public, we are generally asking lots of questions in our heads first. Should I already know the answer to this? What will other people think and how will they react? Am I going to look silly for doing this? All of these are natural human thoughts and worries, but they are also very **UNHELPFUL** when it comes to learning and finding things out.

As any scientist will tell you, the foundation of our work is the ability to ask good questions. First you have to work out what the right questions are (which is easier said than done!) and then you have to find a way to explore them (often by running experiments).

If scientists spent all their time worrying about looking silly or getting things wrong, then very little progress would ever be achieved. In science, getting it wrong and receiving answers you don't expect is all part of the process, as this helps you to experiment.

Which leaves us with another paradox to solve. Being curious and asking lots of questions is one of the best ways to learn and improve. But doing that can be difficult. It exposes us to the judgement and even ridicule of other people. It means putting ourselves out there, raising our hand and speaking out loud the question that is turning over in our head.

This was an area in which I thrived when I was younger. My autism meant that I had **MORE** questions about the world around me, and was also less worried than my peers about what other people might think of me for asking them. I would just ask away: why did you pair that shirt with those shoes, why is he chewing so loudly, why does this person have a weird voice and why is that chair orange? Sometimes people would laugh, or blush, or mostly roll their eyes, but I just carried on. I really wanted to know.

What I realise now is this inability to be embarrassed was my superpower. It allowed me to ask the questions that other people were never brave enough to say out loud.

It meant I could always be exploring and discovering: honing my scientific method from a young age.

In fact, it made me feel a little bit like a computer program. Because the algorithm doesn't get embarrassed. It doesn't feel self-conscious or experience peer pressure. It just keeps crunching data and answering questions until it reaches the answer it has been programmed to find.

And we can perhaps all learn something from that, about the need to ask questions, which is so important in all our lives for many reasons:

QUESTIONS help us to understand things we don't immediately 'get'. Having a concept explained can be so much easier than trying to work it out ourselves from a textbook or online article. By asking questions, we can start a conversation, focus on the bits we don't understand and put things in our own words. They are one of the best tools for learning we have.

QUESTIONS allow us to challenge things we don't feel to be right or fair. Sometimes in a group situation, people can remain quiet about a

problem simply because no one else is speaking up about it. This creates a silent form of peer pressure: when everyone is keeping quiet, we assume they must be happy and that it would be disruptive or impolite to point out the problem ourselves. In these situations, it is harder to ask the question, but also more important to find the courage to do so.

QUESTIONS also help us to be sceptical – to have some level of doubt about what we read or are told. Just like an algorithm, we spend our whole lives taking in information – or ingesting data, in computer science terms. But not all of that data will be accurate or true. We shouldn't believe everything we read or hear, especially on the Internet. Sometimes that information will be untruthful or deliberately misleading. Or it might be presented in a certain way to emphasise one side of an argument while taking focus away from another. Sometimes it will be trying to convince you that you need this new thing or that you should like or dislike that one. The same thing might happen at school: if you hear a rumour about one of your classmates, that doesn't make it true. Yet often people will share stories they have no evidence for except 'someone told me'. Most likely, somebody told somebody who told somebody who told you, and the story got more and more extreme (and less and less true) along the way!

When you're reading something online, especially on social media, always think twice about it. I ask myself: is the information from a source I trust, and should I believe it without double-checking? Does the account sharing that information have something to gain from misleading people? Is there a risk involved in what is being asked of me (like sharing personal information, which you definitely *shouldn't do* unless you are very sure it's safe)?

Any scientist will tell you that the same basic data (information) can be presented in lots of different ways that would lead you to think different things. Being sceptical is one of the best ways to be an independent thinker: someone who comes to their own conclusions about things, processing and using the information around them but also really *thinking* about it.

So remember, always ask yourself what is **REALLY** going on, question whether you should trust a new piece of information (especially if it sounds too good to be true) and double-check if you are unsure. It's what scientists do!

THE CONFIDENCE TRICK

Hopefully by now you'll agree that questions are really important, and an essential part of how we think our way through life's small and big problems.

Even better, they can also help us with another essential life skill: confidence, the ability to believe in yourself, that you are good at something and will be able to succeed.

Confidence is a tricky thing, because too little of it is a problem, but so is too much. We need just the right amount so that we believe in ourselves without becoming overconfident (in a way that leads us to make errors, skip steps, not check our work or not consider what others in our team think).

Confidence can be one of the tougher things to deal with growing up. It's easy to *lose* confidence when someone makes a mean remark or we do less well than we expected on a test. Sometimes negative experiences **FEEL** so much bigger and more important than all the good and brilliant things about us as a person.

I used to have to deal with this a lot, as someone living in a world that never felt designed for me. For years, I asked myself if all the people who said there was something wrong with me were right. To prove that *they* were wrong, I had to learn to find confidence in who I was and how I was.

What I learned is that you **BUILD** up confidence in all sorts of little ways. It's about reminding yourself what you are good at and finding small ways to prove it every day. It can be asking for someone else's opinion about something to back up your own (or help you change your mind). And it helps to remember that things that *seem* important (like that spelling test) will be forgotten about a few days later.

I was also taught a neat exercise that can be helpful if you have had a knock to your confidence – it's a good way of getting in touch with your senses if you are feeling anxious or panicky.

GET IN TOUCH WITH YOUR SENSES

AN EXERCISE FOR FINDING CALM:

NAME FIVE THINGS IN

THE ROOM YOU CAN SEE,

FOUR YOU CAN TOUCH,

THREE YOU CAN HEAR,

TWO YOU CAN SMELL AND

ONE THAT YOU CAN TELL

A STORY ABOUT.

Throughout our lives, most of us will be walking a tightrope between having too much confidence and too little. In some situations we'll completely lack belief in ourselves, but in others we might be overconfident and stumble by not working hard enough.

As we attempt this balancing act, computers provide a surprising but really useful guide! In some ways they are very confident – without any of the emotional self-doubt and uncertainty that we can feel as human beings. But in other ways they are the opposite: they don't assume that a certain answer is true. Instead they keep on crunching the data they have been programmed to look at, and they keep using it to improve the accuracy of their results.

That's a good model for us all to think about: believe in yourself, but don't make too many assumptions or stop listening to new evidence. Always be willing to change the way you think when you receive new or better information (like, maybe the friend you play netball with has suddenly got quite a bit taller, and you should be passing them the ball more often).

Being **CONFIDENT** often means asking questions about things you don't know or understand, or which you want to understand in more detail. Have confidence in your instincts but also keep checking, like the computer is coded to do. Animals in the wild are conditioned to do this as well, using all five senses to scan their surroundings for sights, sounds or smells that might mean danger.

Above all, remember that being clever doesn't mean having all the answers.

A confident person is one who is **BRAVE** enough to ask the **QUESTION**, rather than pretending they already know the answer.

Now you might be wondering, does this mean we need to be more like computers? Which is a *good* question, to which my answer is both **YES** and **NO**.

Because, in lots of important ways, we are nothing like computers. As humans, we are defined by our feelings, our relationships, our creativity and our ability to break the rules as well as follow them.

In comparison to our human perspective, the computer's view on the world is very narrow. After all, it can't see, taste, smell or really experience things. It doesn't have our ability to look at a question from all angles and in unusual ways. Everything in it was put there by humans. It is extremely powerful when it comes to crunching data, but in other ways it is very limited.

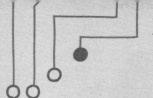

But it does have one real strength that we can try to emulate. It keeps going. It keeps asking. It keeps checking. I can promise you that no computer program has ever been too embarrassed to ask another question. And nor should you be.

So when it comes to the messy business of wading through the data of our everyday lives, we definitely have something important to learn from computers.

That lesson? There is always more information to process, always more to discover – and there is never anything to lose by asking your next question.

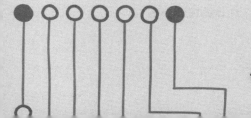

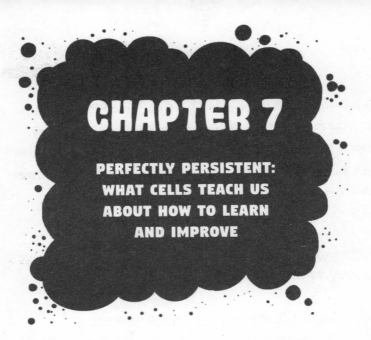

CHAPTER 7

PERFECTLY PERSISTENT: WHAT CELLS TEACH US ABOUT HOW TO LEARN AND IMPROVE

Now we've spent all that time talking about questions, let's start this chapter with one. If you want, try finding a responsible adult to ask it to.

HOW MANY cells are contained in a fully grown human body?

Remember that cells are our body's building blocks: the microscopic bits that combine to form everything on the outside (like skin, hair, teeth and nails), and all the important stuff on the inside (our blood, organs, muscles and nerves).

So how many cells does it take to make that body work – to make our organs whir away, our blood pump, our bones hold steady and our muscles move?

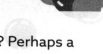

A few hundred, maybe? A few thousand? Perhaps a million? Go on, ask someone and see what they say.

And then **SHOCK** them by telling them the real answer. Which is one that you definitely don't want to be counting on your fingers.

The answer is that the average adult human body has **THIRTY TRILLION** cells in it.

That's 30,000,000,000,000. Thirteen zeros.

This is an *average* number, so it will be different for each individual. Someone with long arms and legs is going to need more cells to cover them with extra skin and muscle and equip them with bigger bones, for example.

But I think we can both agree that it is a **VERY LARGE** number indeed, and not one that anyone has ever reached when counting sheep at night.

Now let me shock you again. Because an adult didn't start out with thirty trillion cells. Nor thirty million. Not thirty thousand. Not even three hundred.

Every one of those thirty trillion cells, every tiny ingredient for all the things that make up the human body, came from **JUST ONE CELL**. That one cell is a special type called a stem cell, which can develop into many other different types of cell (a process which occurs in other species and plants as well as humans). So that first cell divides up, with one becoming two, two splitting into four, four turning into eight and so on. And eventually, every one of these cell divisions added up to make thirty trillion, creating a fully fledged adult human complete with their own toenails and earlobes.

Which is a pretty remarkable thing when you stop to think about it. Because all the different parts of us – everything from skin and blood to bone and muscle, nerves, bits of the brain and the soles of our feet – actually came from exactly the same starting point. How cool is that!

Perhaps even more cool is that we continue to benefit from stem cells as we grow up, and even after our bodies have stopped growing. Our hair and nails still grow, new skin grows to replace the stuff that we scrape off when we take a tumble, our blood supply is constantly replenishing itself and our immune system (the thing that deals with threats to the body like infection) updates itself.

In fact, different cells in different organs replace themselves at different rates. Some cells take days to replace (white blood cells that make your immunity strong, stomach cells, skin cells), some take months (bone, pancreas), some take many, many years (heart, eye lens cells), and some stay with you for a lifetime (brain cells). Stem cells are doing all that work in your body right now as you are reading this. Thumbs up to them!

That's all quite interesting and cool, but why am I telling you about it? What do the little geniuses that are stem cells have to teach us about ourselves?

I think it's a simple but very important lesson: **EVERYTHING** has to start **SOMEWHERE**.

That could be a hobby, a friendship, a skill you want to develop or an achievement you want to accomplish. It could be about learning to play a musical instrument, getting better at your favourite game, making a new friend or being able to run or swim faster.

Whatever it may be, like the stem cell, *we have to start somewhere*. Because all of the things we value most in life are done **SLOWLY**. There are no shortcuts or easy wins.

It takes WORK, EFFORT and PRACTICE to get better at anything. It doesn't just fall from the sky or jump out from the screen – we have to choose to START the engine!

The good things in life are only good because we have to work to get them, we make mistakes along the way, then we pick ourselves up and start over in this crazy experiment that is human life. This process won't always make us feel happy or fulfilled. Sometimes it will be difficult, annoying or upsetting. But these are moments that will pass rather than feelings that will last forever. We need to take them all in our stride and remember to keep going and not give up easily.

That is where we can look to our own bodies for clues. Because, if anything proves how much can be achieved by something small but determined – given enough time to work, evolve and repeat – it is the stem cell.

These marvels of creation show what is possible. The question is, how can we follow their example?

STARTING SMALL

Whatever it is you want to achieve, we all know that one of the hardest parts is getting started. Like if I want to clean my house, I start noticing all the things that are wrong: I'm about to run out of loo roll, there's no milk to put in my tea and there's a pile of clothes on the floor that keeps getting bigger every time I look at it.

Silly as it sounds, I can get overwhelmed by this. I don't know whether to start with the milk or the dirty clothes. Because I have too many choices, I often end up freezing completely and not doing anything at all. Sometimes I'm too scared to even open the fridge (imagine that!). Once or twice I've put the dirty socks in the freezer, just so they would be out of sight.

It's easy to get intimidated when we don't know where or how to start on something. Or perhaps you get worried because the *end*, the goal you are trying to achieve, feels so far distant.

If a room is so messy that it is going to take hours to tidy, then the thought of all that work can be tiring before you've even folded a single T-shirt. Or if you know that it's

going to take weeks, months and years of practice to get better at playing an instrument, that can be just as off-putting. It feels easier to not start at all!

This is why getting **STARTED** is the hard part. It's easier to give up before we have taken the first steps on a journey, when it feels like we have nothing to lose.

But imagine if the first couple of stem cells that eventually turned into your eyes, ears, bones and muscles had said the same thing? What if they had decided that having a nap in the embryo was a better idea than getting to work?

When I'm in a situation like this, I like to think about stem cells. They are a great reminder of how far you can go if you have the courage and the commitment to get started.

If the stem cell can begin at one and end at thirty trillion, how much do you think you can achieve if you give yourself the chance to do something wonderful? Go on, just take that **FIRST** step. I promise the next one will be easier.

Stem cells can be our guide as we do the difficult work of starting new and exciting things.

But, little geniuses that they are, they can also do so much more, like showing us how we can achieve progress as we go along the journey.

If the first lesson of the stem cell is that every end has a start, then the second is that, on the way, things get complicated and wonderfully twisty.

While all cells start from the same source, once they get into the business of division, they stop behaving in the same way. There are different types of stem cells that are responsible for different things, like developing new tissue for our organs or growing our hair and fingernails.

This is called **SPECIALISATION**: as the cells divide and develop, they also take on individual characteristics and specific roles, much like people breaking off into different subject sets or friendship groups. At this stage, the cells are no longer just happily

145

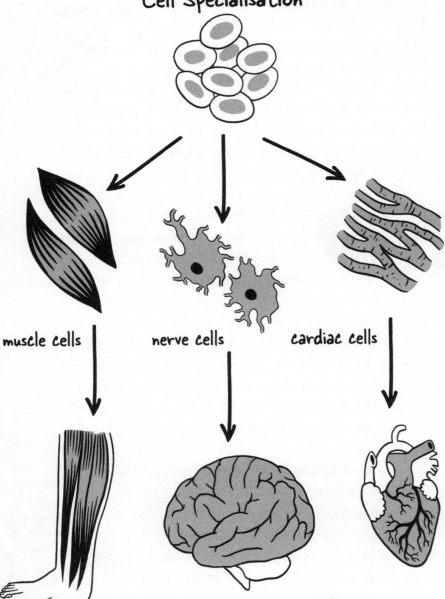

dividing away without a care in the world; they are doing a specific job that they have evolved in a particular way to do.

I think that's a bit like the way we change and develop as we get better at a skill in life. Like playing the piano, something I have always loved to do. A person who has been doing this for several years and is now starting to play more complex pieces isn't just a *better* piano player than they used to be. They're also a different person from the one who first sat down in front of a keyboard. The way they listen, think, use their hands and read music has changed.

All these skills have become specialised for the job of piano playing, just as some stem cells evolve in a specific way that allows them to produce red or white blood cells in the body.

Our bodies and brains are constantly undergoing this process of specialisation: getting better in particular ways in order to meet a certain challenge. For example, someone will have better hand–eye co-ordination (the ability to respond to moving objects) if they are a football or hockey goalkeeper who practises every week.

Sometimes these changes aren't so much about improvement (getting better at something) as adaptation. As I've already told you, when I was a child I did things like squeaking and jerking my head to get out all the thoughts and feelings I couldn't control. Aged twenty-eight, I still get the same waves of emotion, but I deal with them differently.

I've taught myself to channel the impulse into something that people find less startling (and which they probably don't notice at all). Instead of suddenly going 'PARP', I will make a few tiny coughs and stroke the collar of my T-shirt or my hair. These give me the same feeling of release without the outward expressions that I couldn't control aged eight.

(Important note: I share this as an example of how we adapt as humans over time, not to say that there was anything wrong with my jerking and squeaking, or that what I do today is any 'better'. It's just my way of making myself feel calm at the same time as helping other people to be comfortable around me. It's different for everyone and nobody gets to say what is or isn't normal body language. You do you!)

In some ways I've had to change, but the world changes too. For reasons you can guess, I have always disliked the way people greet each other with hugs, handshakes and kisses on the cheek. I hate having my personal space intruded on, and I don't know what kind of germs the kissers and huggers may be carrying.

For most of my life, this meant lots of people thought I was unsociable and rude. But then the Covid-19 pandemic came around, and I found it reassuring to discover that there were others who agreed with me, who weren't so keen on shaking hands or sharing kisses with people they had just met.

It was the same with smoking, which used to be allowed in restaurants when I was your age. For me, this seemed like an obviously bad thing, the horrible fumes stinging my eyes and the smell invading my nostrils. It seemed totally confusing and unfair that this could be allowed. So when smoking indoors was banned for health reasons, it felt fantastic. My concern hadn't been me being weird, but was supported by a valid set of reasons that more and more people started to agree with over time.

It's a funny old world, and sometimes it moves towards you if you give it long enough. First they ridicule you, then they agree with you and later they might even copy you.

PRACTICE MAKES PERFECT

As we adapt, change and improve throughout our lives, one thing usually holds true. We tend to get **BETTER** at the things we need to be good at. And that happens because we are spending a lot of time practising them.

When we practise something enough, it becomes so familiar that we start to do it by instinct – without having to think about it. The pianist's fast fingers and the goalkeeper's quick reactions are all a product of careful and consistent practice. So when you see someone or something that looks 'perfect' on TV or on social media, like a dancer or singer, remember that what isn't shown is the process of getting there – all the hard work it took to get that good.

These people have earned their evolution by doing the thing they do until they no longer have to think through all the steps involved. They just know where their hands are meant to be on the keyboard or where the ball is going to go when it hurtles towards the goal. It becomes second nature to them.

We can't stay as the embryonic stem cell who is always kicking a ball or reading a book for the first time. We need to develop our skills, our knowledge and our expertise – the human equivalent of cell division and specialisation. Some of this 'division' happens as a natural part of growing up: we learn to smile, walk and talk simply by taking in what is around us as babies and toddlers, copying the example of others and making use of our growing bodies. We go through all these complex stages of development before we have the ability to form a conscious thought – to think about what we are doing and why.

But as we get older, reaching the age you are now, things change. We can think for ourselves, which means we have choices. We can decide to do something or *not* to do it. Progress becomes less a matter of biology and more one of personal choice.

We won't improve our physical fitness unless we train. We won't improve our test scores unless we do our homework. And we won't get better at playing a musical instrument unless we practise.

Here's another thing: the better we get at any of these things, the harder we have to work to improve. We've done the achievable parts that almost anyone can do, like learning to read music or getting fit enough to run around the pitch ten times. Now the question is, do we want to put in the effort to get *really* good at something? And that's hard, because it requires more effort, we are taking smaller steps, and our progress can feel less significant.

That might sound daunting, but we also have to accept that the best achievements in life are usually the ones we have to work hard to get, which aren't handed to us on a plate. If you struggle with spelling but then come top of the class in a test, it's going to feel better than if you are naturally good at it – what a win! For me today, training a puppy has been a lot of hard work, but when she does her business in the right place for a change, I want to punch the air in celebration on her behalf!

Which leads us to the point I think is really important. **PROGRESS** in our lives isn't about **PERFECTION**. No one is going to be right every time, save every goal or never miss a note on the piano (though sometimes a tune sounds better when you do!).

As we practise hard and work to get better, we are going to make mistakes. These are just a part of life and it's so much healthier to accept this fact than to be too hard on ourselves when something goes wrong.

In science, this mindset is essential to the process of investigating how things work and then making them work better. Trial and error teaches us what can go right, what can go wrong and how to do things differently. Failed experiments are as useful to the scientist as ones that 'succeed'.

Which isn't to say that they're fun. When I couldn't do something 'perfectly' the first time, I would often get frustrated, moody and upset without being able to explain why. It's annoying when things go wrong, but that's exactly why you have to remember that not everything can go right.

Even if we haven't 'succeeded', we have probably learned something through our 'failure'. It may have helped us to see the world slightly differently. Or it might have been a step on the road to eventual success.

Here's an example: your parents probably own a vacuum cleaner, and it might be a Dyson, one of the fancy models. The person who created this, James Dyson, is one of the most famous inventors in the UK. And it took him over **FIVE THOUSAND** attempts to get the very first model right. But all those 'failures' helped him to perfect something that became a massive success.

In the end, progress is about **PRACTICE**. It's about trying, working and making many small improvements until we can do something that we couldn't before. It's about making ourselves better, smarter and stronger, one small step at a time: finding our own unique path as we grow up, and taking setbacks in our stride.

And you know what? That stays true all the way through life. It's true for those of you reading this book. It's *definitely* true for me writing it. And it's true for our parents and teachers. We are all works in progress, constantly changing inside and out. We need to improve and we're capable of evolution if we put the effort in. Which is the stem cell's final and perhaps most important lesson. It never stops dividing. And nor should we.

CHAPTER 8

PERFECTLY WRONG: WHAT SCIENCE TEACHES US ABOUT HOW TO DISAGREE

I don't know about you, but I used to find school mornings really hard. There's so much to do in so little time. You have to get out of bed, eat breakfast, brush your teeth and check you've packed the right folders in your rucksack.

You can't find your socks, your shirt has a stain on it and your shoes are scuffed. And that's before you even start to think about whether you've got any clean PE kit.

All that, and you haven't even left the house yet!

I used to think about it like a video game, hitting X to move myself from one task to the next, worried that if I didn't complete them all in the

specific order I had planned, I would malfunction and end up at school in my Bugs Bunny slippers.

Sometimes this video game approach helped, but the real boss battle of every school morning was getting dressed.

I hated having to put on the tights that were part of my school uniform, which pinched and restricted me in all the wrong places. I didn't like my shoes. And, strange as it sounds, I was scared of buttons. Even touching the ones on my shirt made me feel like I was going to be sick.

This was a big problem, especially for my poor mum, who had to deal with the daily struggle to get me dressed and out of the door. But the uniform, much as I hated it, wasn't something that I could say no to. The whole point of a uniform is that everyone wears it. It makes everyone the same and means one person isn't wearing tatty old trainers while the kid next to them is in designer shoes.

Even though my school did lots of things to help me feel comfortable and included, like giving me a personal helper and time out of lessons when I felt overwhelmed, letting me break the rules by not wearing uniform couldn't be one of them.

So, with my mum's assistance, I devised an answer. I wore the tights, with holes cut in them that couldn't be seen but which made me feel much comfier. And the buttons were taken off my school shirts and replaced with poppers, which felt much easier on my fingers and didn't make me want to gag.

This was a **COMPROMISE**: a solution that suits the most important needs of everyone and lets the less important needs go. I was wearing the uniform and not breaking any rules. But I had also managed to avoid the parts of that rule that made me feel most uncomfortable. It was good for everyone – what we call a win–win.

Compromise is just one of the ways we can respond when we encounter something that is a big part of life: *people, rules or ideas that we disagree with.*

It could be something as trivial as what music is going to be playing in the car on the school run. Or it could be something serious, like a disagreement about how to treat another person with kindness and respect. What one person finds funny might easily be offensive to another, which may leave you wondering if you need to pick a side – and how to do so.

DISAGREEMENT is a part of all our lives, something we must learn to manage and feel comfortable with (which is hard, because it can often feel very *un*comfortable).

Of course, nobody wants to spend their whole day having arguments. But we also can't avoid the fact that people are different: we have our own tastes, views on the world and principles that we believe to be important. Standing up for these things is going to lead to disagreements with other people, even if they are only very small ones.

The **GOOD** news is that disagreement doesn't have to mean falling out with your friends and family. It's perfectly possible to disagree in a polite and constructive way that avoids people getting angry and being nasty to each other. Done carefully, disagreement can actually be **HELPFUL**.

To learn why, we should look to a place where disagreement happens by design: the world of science. In the process of scientific **DISCOVERY**, where you are trying to find answers and solutions that may or may not exist, disagreement is the fuel on which everything runs.

Scientists need to disagree with each other to debate different ideas and challenge each other with alternative viewpoints, in order to make **PROGRESS**. They need someone to stand on the other side of the argument and point out the bits they haven't thought of or the problems they haven't taken into account.

Some of the most important scientific discoveries have been matters of huge controversy (public debate and disagreement). Today we know and accept that Earth revolves around the sun. The time taken for this to happen (365 days plus a few hours) is how we mark calendar years. But in the 1600s, one of the scientists who argued for this theory (because it was still just a theory back then), an Italian astronomer called Galileo, caused so much controversy that he was put on trial because his science went against what was written in the Bible.

If we didn't have scientists who were brave enough to stand up for their research in this way, to **DISAGREE** with what they were taught and seek out better answers, we would never have come so far or discovered so much.

Science teaches us that disagreements don't have to be disastrous, and they don't need to be unpleasant. They can actually be an important way of discovering new things while expressing ourselves. Plus they help us to see the world through other people's eyes as well as our own.

So let's take a leaf out of science's book and explore how disagreements happen, why they matter and how to do them better.

LOOKING THROUGH THE KALEIDOSCOPE

But before we can get to scientific solutions, we need to understand the problem. Why is it that we have disagreements? I think the answer lies inside one of my favourite gizmos: a kaleidoscope.

If you've ever looked through a kaleidoscope, then you know it's a weird and wonderful place inside that tiny

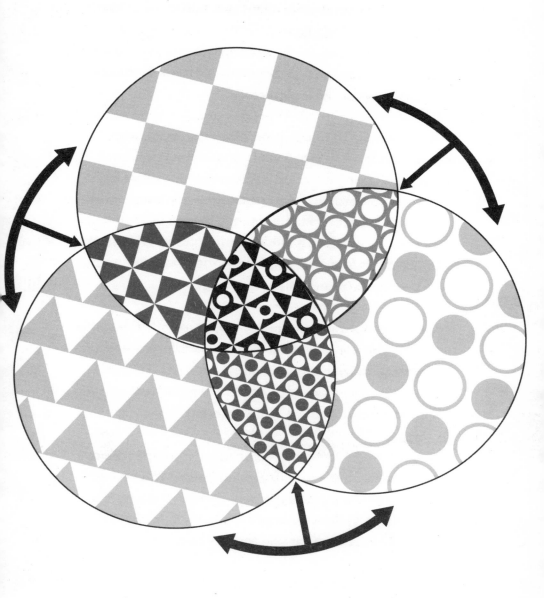

tube. The really fun part is when you turn or twist it and your view completely changes. The reason for that is that you have altered the angle of the mirrors inside the tube, changing the way the light bounces off them and back to our eyes – a whole new picture.

That's how I like to think about disagreements: we are handing the kaleidoscope from person to person, everyone is giving it a good twist and every single one of us sees something different. But the contents of the kaleidoscope haven't changed; only the way we look at them has. It's a bit like a film you thought was hilarious but your sister found boring, or a singer that your friend loves but who you secretly find cringe.

You are both forming an opinion about *exactly the same thing*. But you are looking at it through different eyes, as people with your own individual interests, likes and dislikes. Like a kaleidoscope that's been twisted, you will end up seeing something quite different.

This is where disagreements can start. Perhaps you *love* country music, but your sibling can't begin to understand why. Maybe they make fun of you for it (in the way that siblings do), just like you might tease them for being really into a cartoon that you think is quite silly.

Neither of you will be able to understand the other person's point of view. You are both *convinced* that you are right, because you are looking through your version of the kaleidoscope and they are looking through theirs.

When you can't actually see what they are seeing (nor they what you are seeing), it can be hard to understand why they might think that way.

So how do we fix these differences in views; these contrasting peeks down the kaleidoscope of life?

I think we need to take a scientific approach. A scientist doesn't automatically say that *this* person is right and *that* person is wrong. Instead, they want to explore *why* they have seen and felt different things, and *what* they can learn from this. They recognise that facts are wobbly, people experience things in their own individual way, and it is better to try and understand different opinions than immediately decide they must be wrong.

This is the first step to getting better at handling disagreement: to understand that someone else might have a very different perspective or opinion from you, and then to recognise *that is absolutely fine*. It **DOESN'T MATTER** if someone else thinks your favourite music is rubbish or can't understand why you would support Spurs. These are opinions, not facts, and they are welcome to keep theirs to themselves.

Even better, because you now have a kaleidoscope in your pocket, you recognise that the person who can't understand your interests or hobbies will have plenty of weird ones of their own. Because we're all looking through the kaleidoscope, and we all see our own unique picture in it.

HAVE BETTER ARGUMENTS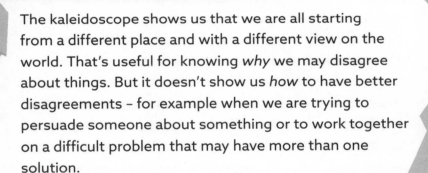

The kaleidoscope shows us that we are all starting from a different place and with a different view on the world. That's useful for knowing *why* we may disagree about things. But it doesn't show us *how* to have better disagreements – for example when we are trying to persuade someone about something or to work together on a difficult problem that may have more than one solution.

For that, we need to turn to science again, to the first step in solving any scientific problem: *define what you are trying to achieve.*

Sounds easy, right? Except this is where a lot of experiments go wrong: by failing to set clear terms right at the beginning. You need to be very precise about *what* you are looking for, *where* you will look for it and *how* you will look (using which scientific theories or methods).

I think this is the mindset we need with disagreements: to understand what we are trying to achieve first, before we open our mouths and start talking over each other.

This is particularly important because there is more than one kind of disagreement, which means there is more than one way to manage disagreements.

Let's look at a few of the different kinds, and how to go about managing them.

DIFFERENCES OF OPINION: WHEN IT'S TIME TO COMPROMISE

There are differences of opinion and taste about things like the music we listen to, hobbies we enjoy and books we like to read. Here, we are unlikely to change anyone's mind: however hard I try, I will probably never convince you that *Pocahontas* is the greatest Disney movie ever (unless you're already a fan). Similarly, when I was six you would *never* have been able to get me to eat any brown food (even chocolate, which meant I disagreed with approximately 99% of people I have ever met).

That's fine, because it would be boring if we all agreed about what's good, interesting, fun or flavoursome. These disagreements also teach us an important lesson. *Don't waste time and energy trying to change someone's mind about something they already have a very strong opinion on.* And if you're tempted to try, then think about how you would feel if someone tried to get you to agree with them that your favourite music was rubbish. You wouldn't! In fact, you would probably dig in your heels even harder to defend the thing you care passionately about.

WRITE DOWN SOMETHING YOU BELIEVE ABOUT SO PASSIONATELY THAT YOU WOULD NEVER CHANGE YOUR MIND ABOUT IT, HOWEVER HARD SOMEONE TRIED TO MAKE YOU.

So what can we do instead?

Rather than starting an argument that is only going to end with bad feelings, try and have a conversation that can lead somewhere useful. And try to understand where the other person is coming from. You might have more in common than you first thought, or you might find yourself compromising and hopefully avoiding an argument.

If, for example, the disagreement is with your brother or sister about what music you are going to play on a long car journey, try a compromise. Both (or all) of you get to be DJ for part of the journey: everyone wins, and everyone loses. And you move from having a disagreement you *can't* resolve (about whose musical taste is better) to one that you *can* (like who gets to go first; maybe you can play Rock, Paper, Scissors to decide, which is one of my favourite ways of negotiating).

These are the disagreements that are all about compromise: respecting that someone else has a very different opinion from you and finding a solution that makes room for all these different needs and viewpoints.

DIFFERENCES OF EXPERIENCE: WHEN YOU NEED EMPATHY

Sometimes a disagreement will not be about personal taste but individual experience.

'It's FUN,' you might say as you dive into a swimming pool and start doing a back crawl, while your friend stands nervously on the edge. Fun for you, but maybe they are scared of the water and always have been.

Or it could be before a spelling test. 'This is EASY,' says the person whose favourite subject is English. But not for someone in the class who may be dyslexic. For them, getting words and letters in the right order is one of the hardest things, even though they probably have a brilliant mind that is clever and creative in all sorts of other ways.

In a similar way, someone with autism may work out the answer to a complex problem more quickly than their classmates, but because their head is spinning with too much information and too many ideas, they can't always form the words to communicate and explain what they are thinking.

These are differences in how we *experience* the world, based on who we are, where we have come from and how our bodies and minds work.

We can't argue these away. There's no way of trying to convince someone who's scared of water that swimming is enjoyable, or someone who struggles with words that a spelling test is going to be easy.

Instead we need **EMPATHY**: to understand that we all experience the world in a unique way. We have different strengths and weaknesses and our own individual hopes and fears.

We should NEVER assume that, just because WE find something EASY, FUN or ENJOYABLE, everyone else will think the same.

Don't try to debate with people about the things they find difficult or scary. Don't tell them it's easy, or fun, or that they just need to get over it.

I know how frustrating and damaging it can be when this happens. When I would get anxious about noises or smells that other people didn't even notice, people would say that I was 'overreacting', 'being dramatic' or even 'crazy'. But this was simply how I experienced the world, something made even more difficult by some people's refusal to show empathy. Just as bad were the teachers who tried forcing me to make eye contact to be 'polite', even though doing so actually caused me pain.

Trying to force other people into seeing and feeling the world as you do isn't just unrealistic and a bad way of solving disagreements. It can actually be harmful to them.

Instead, I would have loved it if my classmates had tried to see the world through my eyes. Tried to understand why I was acting a certain way and to be supportive. It's not hard for us to say to someone else, 'You're doing really well' or 'Let me help you'. And it's so much more useful to hear than, 'What's the problem? Everyone else can do it just fine.'

Helping and supporting the people around us, instead of judging them or arguing with them because they experience the world differently, is the **KIND** thing to do. That's the **MAGIC** of kindness – it isn't hard, it's totally free and it can make a huge difference to everyone around you.

DIFFERENCES OF PRINCIPLE: WHEN IT'S TIME TO STAND UP FOR YOURSELF (OR SOMEONE ELSE)

So far we've looked at different types of disagreement when it pays to be friendly, kind and understanding. But there are situations where this doesn't always work: when someone is being rude or unfair to you, or even discriminating against you.

This was something I experienced a lot growing up, because of my autism and behaviour that looked 'weird' to other people. Other kids made fun of me. I was told I belonged in a zoo. Strangers would stare at me in the street. And some teachers punished me for being disruptive to their classes because I was trying to learn in my own way.

Perhaps you have experienced something similar. If you're a girl, maybe you feel that you've been discouraged from playing sport or pursuing your passion for maths and science. Maybe you feel that people have looked at or treated you differently because of the colour of your skin. Maybe, like me, you are neurodivergent, with a brain that works differently, and have faced odd looks and annoying questions because of it.

And even if none of these things have happened to you personally, they almost certainly *have* to at least some of your friends and the people you care about.

These are the toughest situations, because they're not ones where someone is disagreeing with you about something that can be debated – like the best way to learn times tables, or whether Ariana Grande is better than Dua Lipa. These are situations where someone is disagreeing with you *as a person:* failing to understand you, not having empathy with the way you experience the world, or even discriminating against you (treating you differently from how they would treat anyone else).

Knowing how to respond in these situations is tricky. Sometimes it may be the right course of action to confront someone directly: to tell them why what they have said or done is wrong and why it has hurt you. But you should only ever do this when it feels safe and sensible to do so.

Often, it will be a better option to tell a teacher or parent what has happened and get their help to deal with the situation. Sometimes we're too upset to talk with the person who is being horrible to us or our friend, and that's completely fine, but a teacher or responsible adult can help you.

The important thing is, when someone has done or said something to make you feel upset or uncomfortable, *don't* bottle up those feelings and hide away. Talk to someone – a friend, a sibling or a trusted adult – and get their help. If you don't, a situation can get worse, and bad feelings can grow and grow until they become overwhelming. If you let unhappy thoughts sit around for long enough without sharing them, then you may start to think that you deserve them (spoiler alert: you do not – you deserve to be understood, heard and treated with respect, and so does everyone else!).

As we discussed when we looked at bullying in chapter 3, when someone is being mean to you, it's usually because they have problems of their own. They might feel angry, jealous of you or insecure about themselves. You're not to blame when someone else chooses to treat you badly.

The best thing you can do is to get **HELP**. At the same time, you also need to know when to stand up for yourself. There will be situations in life where people are trying to get you to do things you don't want to do: maybe they are planning something naughty and want you to be part of it.

And there are also situations where people are trying to *stop* you from doing things that you *do* want to do: like when I was picking my GCSE subjects and the school tried to make me do less science and more languages.

In both cases, it's important to have a strong sense of what you believe is the right thing to do *and then to stick to it*. A pretty good rule for life is that you shouldn't let other people talk you into doing things that you think are a bad idea. And you shouldn't let people talk you out of doing things if you are absolutely certain that you both want and are able to do them.

I knew that science was in my heart, so I insisted on doing all the science GCSEs I could. Now I'm grown up and working as a scientist, that feels like it was a good decision!

For me, it's a reminder of the power of sticking up for yourself. When you know that you are right, or that something matters, you shouldn't let someone persuade you otherwise unless they have an extremely good reason. We have instincts, those inner feelings about what to do, for a good reason. Trust your instincts and don't be easily convinced to go against them.

Hopefully I've shown in this chapter why disagreements are important, as well as some different ways of going about managing them.

Sometimes we need to **RECOGNISE** when and why there is a disagreement, and find ways to resolve it through compromise or by showing empathy.

And at other times we need to **DEFEND** the things we care about and refuse to let other people walk all over us.

Done properly, disagreement is a healthy and natural part of life.

But remember to **THINK** like a scientist would. First, assess and understand the situation you are in (*why* do we disagree and about *what*?). Then pick an approach to fit the situation (for example, 'I'm going to try and find a compromise here'; 'I'm going to accept that my sister finds this harder than I do and try to help'; 'I'm going to stand up for a friend who is being picked on'; or 'I'm going to get help because I can't solve this one on my own').

When someone disagrees with us or criticises us, it can be **HARD** to deal with. We're tempted to take it personally and argue straight back, leading to an emotional or even angry confrontation.

What follows should be calmer, friendlier and more **USEFUL**.

And if you disagree with any of that, I'd love to hear about it!

MY TIPS WOULD BE:

Take a breath. **AHHH, BETTER** already.

DON'T say the first thing that comes into your head.

If it's **STILL** bothering you, write down your thoughts or draw them. This is something that has **ALWAYS** helped me when I'm in the midst of a frustrating disagreement!

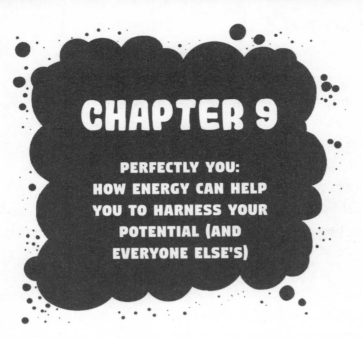

CHAPTER 9

PERFECTLY YOU: HOW ENERGY CAN HELP YOU TO HARNESS YOUR POTENTIAL (AND EVERYONE ELSE'S)

Growing up, one of my favourite games was also one of the simplest. It didn't require anything except a set of swings in the park and the shoes we were already wearing. We'd rock back and forward on the swing,

gaining speed. The game was then to flick a shoe off our feet, as far back over the playground fence as possible. Very imaginatively, we called it 'Shoe-ey'.

It's a great feeling when you know that you've 'hit' a good shot and that your shoe is about to go soaring high over that fence (although, please, only try this in places where you're not at risk of hitting someone with it!).

Shoe-ey is also a good science demonstration. Because, as you flick your foot and send your shoe flying, an interesting bit of physics is happening. Through the motion of your foot, you are converting what is called the *potential energy* of your shoe into the *kinetic energy* that helps it to move.

Then, when it reaches the top of its flight and starts to fall, that is converted again into *gravitational potential energy* – enabling the downward force of gravity that we discussed in chapter 3, the one that pulls things back to earth.

The game reveals a funny but important bit of physics that we all need to understand. Every single object, just sitting there minding its own business, has this potential energy stored inside it.

A cat curled up in its basket might look lazy and comfortable, but it is actually *full* of potential energy: ready to move and pounce. And when it spots a bird in the garden or smells a tin of tuna being opened from across the kitchen, it will leap out of the basket – its potential energy becoming kinetic energy all of a sudden.

It's the same with a mug of tea sitting on the table next to you. If you accidentally knock it over, then you have released its gravitational potential energy and it will fall to the ground. (This is why I often work sitting or lying on the floor, where accidents are less likely to happen.)

Literally everything in the universe, everything you

can see and touch around you, whether it's a living or inanimate object, has potential energy.

But the amount of this energy isn't always the same.

A tennis ball that you drop from above your head is going to fall to the ground at a faster speed than one you hold out by your side. It has *more* gravitational potential energy thanks to the effort you put in to lift it up in the first place (working against gravity to do so).

Similarly, you are going to bounce higher on a trampoline if you jump really hard on it – because you are compressing the springs inside it further, increasing their potential energy and allowing them to propel you back up higher.

We call this energy **ELASTIC** potential, and you can think of it as a measure of how springy something is. (It can also be a useful way of thinking about our energy as people: because I can find big events tiring, I might try not to see anyone the previous day so that I have more elastic potential for when I really need it.)

For me, learning about potential energy was an important part of understanding my own potential as a person.

The phrase 'you have so much potential' really used to annoy me (and still does!) because I didn't understand what it meant and it didn't seem to chime with how lots of people treated me: as someone who was never going to achieve anything because I was so obviously 'weird' and couldn't concentrate on anything or do as I was told.

Potential energy was much more **FRIENDLY**, and helped to explain things. It taught me that, just like every *thing* contains potential energy, so too does every one of *us*.

That's a literal scientific statement: our bodies are massive stores of the energy we need to function, something we are topping up every time we eat a meal or snack.

But potential energy is also an idea with wider meaning. Because we all have potential, every single one of us. We all have the ability to do interesting things with our lives, to be successful, to have fun, to learn things and to love and help other people.

Working out our own potential is one of the biggest adventures in life, and something that continues well into adulthood. We are all trying to find out what we want to do, what we enjoy and how to leave a positive mark on the world and people around us. And because we are all individuals, with our own unique differences and bits of weirdness, this is something that only we can do for ourselves.

So in this chapter, I'm going to look at how the idea of potential energy can help us define and ultimately unleash our potential as people.

POTENTIAL: IT'S PERSONAL

Our potential starts with **US**, which immediately leads us to a problem: the very human habit of comparing ourselves to other people!

We all do it. For example, I bet you have often looked at what your friends and classmates are doing, and focused only on what they are really good at (especially if it's something you're *not* good at)?

If they run faster than you, finish homework quicker or have more people sitting with them at lunch, it can make you feel bad. Even worse, when you're focusing so much on other people, you forget all the things that make you a brilliant and interesting person, and you look only at the negative comparison. 'He can do this and I can't.' 'She's great at that and I'm not, so what's the point of even trying?'

This is a very unhelpful way of looking at the world. It's also an **INACCURATE** way of thinking about ourselves.

It means we think less of our own potential because we are spending so much time worrying about everyone else's.

And it doesn't allow us to consider how *different* our potential and abilities are from other people's.

The fact is that we are **ALL** good at some things and not so good at others. Often, this is just a random fact of the genes we inherited from our parents.

For example, some people have very fast reactions – if something drops near them, they'll probably catch it. Some people have a natural 'ear' for music: they can sing the right note without being given it first on the piano (we call this perfect pitch). Others have a particularly advanced sense of smell (it's called *hyperosmia*, and it's useful if you want to work as a chef or in the perfume business).

Our differences as people can exist from birth, or they can develop from the environment we grow up in: the people, places and influences that surround us.

If we have a maths teacher for a parent, then we're probably going to get up to speed quicker with algebra and long division. Or if someone has lots of books at home and their parents read to them from an early age, they're probably going to develop more quickly as a reader themselves. Some people have advantages that others don't, which isn't fair, but it doesn't make them better people. It just makes them lucky.

Here's the point: our potential as individuals is the product of all sorts of chance factors, from the genetics we are made of to the environment we grow up in and how the world chooses to treat people who look, sound and behave as we do.

Potential is **PERSONAL**: we can't have anyone else's, and they can't have ours. No more than we can swap natural hair colours or earlobes.

In life, there are some things we just aren't built for, and that's fine. It's reality, just like a brick can never have elastic potential energy, however hard you try to use it like a spring.

Don't feel bad or worry about this. **FOCUS** on the things you enjoy and excel at instead. Nurture *your* potential and don't let it be overshadowed by that of others. Remember that there are things *you* know which they *don't*, and things *you* can do which they *can't*.

We all suffer at times in our life from a lack of self-confidence, which can make it hard to see or believe in our potential as people. But we *have* to keep trying, because that is the only way we will truly discover ourselves and work out what we are going to be brilliant at. In my life, I had to fight to pursue my studies and career in science. Some of my teachers didn't want me to focus so much on science subjects. Later, some people said I wouldn't have the concentration or focus needed to be a professional scientist, because my ADHD makes me jump around so much between different ideas.

But I ignored these opinions because I *knew* that science was my guiding light. It just spoke to me and made sense in a way nothing else ever had. It was clear to me from the first day I opened a science book that it had the *potential* to be a massive piece of my personal jigsaw. I've stuck to that view ever since, and never once regretted it.

It doesn't matter what you decide you are going to do in your life (and it might be years before you've worked it out, so take your time!). Maybe you're not going to be a maths genius or a brilliant athlete. Don't sweat it – there are so many wonderful parts of your life that you haven't even thought about yet.

So DON'T beat yourself up if you're not top of the class or first pick for the team. And DON'T stop searching for the things you will love and be brilliant at. They EXIST, I promise.

DOING THE WORK

Here's another thing about potential: it's sitting there, waiting to be unlocked, but it's not going to do the job itself.

People will sometimes say that things are 'meant to happen', but nothing ever did without someone taking some kind of action first.

It's like how a ball won't start rolling down a slide unless you push it off the top first: it's full of potential energy, but it requires that kinetic boost to get started.

It needs someone to give it that nudge, applying a force that will convert its potential energy into something it can use to get moving.

There is a word in physics for describing this process – the application of force that leads to energy being transformed from one form into another. It is called **WORK**. (And yes, that's a technical term.)

Work is what happens when you lift a tennis ball above your head to drop it (or toss it up to serve in a tennis match). Because gravity wants the ball to go down to earth, you are having to apply force to push or throw it upwards, in defiance of gravity. You are having to work.

By doing so, you are converting the ball's potential energy into kinetic energy as it moves, and then gravitational potential energy as it falls back down again.

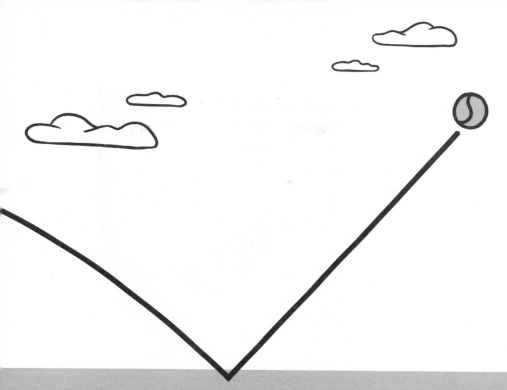

Without this work to convert its potential energy – lifting the tennis ball off the floor or throwing it up out of your hand – nothing would happen.

And it is *exactly the same for us* as we go about our lives.

Unless we *do the work*, nothing happens. We remain exactly where we are. We haven't done anything with our potential.

So we have to push ourselves to start turning that potential energy into something real and useful. Humans throughout history have been doing this to turn good ideas into world-changing inventions. Our world would look incredibly different today if an engineer called Thomas Savery hadn't worked out that you could use the steam from boiling water as a form of energy: a discovery that led to the development of engines, not unlike the ones you see in a car today!

The work we do to unlock potential might not change the world like Savery did, but it's still pretty important to us.

Work might be forcing yourself to learn something that seems boring, because it will help you to tackle the more interesting bits. Even as a science and maths obsessive, there are theories and methods that never chimed with me, but I made myself learn them because I knew they were important ingredients in the overall recipe. Just like flour doesn't taste nice on its own, but you can't bake a cake without it. I didn't *enjoy* this work, but it did help me to unlock my potential as a scientist, so I'm grateful that I did it.

'Work' isn't just about your schoolwork. It's also about how you become a better, more **COMPASSIONATE** person. It could mean listening more carefully to your family and friends to understand things that may be bothering them, and how you can help. It might be about supporting a cause you care about, for example by raising money through a readathon.

Work, in this context, is simply what we do to get the ball rolling and then to keep it going. No one should pretend that this is easy. The 'gravity' in our lives is that it's easier to do nothing: not to do that extra bit of reading or homework, not to do something we find challenging, not to offer to help someone.

But we are better people when we push against that force and **DO** the work. We get **BETTER** at the things we enjoy doing, whether that's playing sport, building models, doing maths problems or baking cakes. We are **KINDER** when we look for ways to help other people without being asked to. And we are **SMARTER** when we keep trying to learn new things. This is how we evolve and live! It's how we discover what we have the potential to be brilliant at.

The important thing isn't to be really good at something straight away. It's having the confidence and curiosity to try, keep trying and keep improving as you go. That, ultimately, is how we **DISCOVER** and fulfil potential.

So potential is personal to you, and it takes work to start converting it into something you can see and feel.

There is also one final point I want to mention, which takes us back to the playground swings where we started this chapter.

Let's say we are all playing a game of Shoe-ey together. It's a competition, but not an entirely fair one. One person is going to have stronger and longer legs than the others, helping them to propel their shoe further.

Another might be sitting on a swing that's closer to the fence, meaning theirs has less distance to travel.

Maybe between my go and yours, the wind will start blowing harder (remember air resistance, from chapter 3?).

In other words, we're not all starting from the same place or playing with the same equipment.

Unfortunately, the same thing is true in life.

There are lots of things that might mean you are starting the game further away from the fence, with shorter legs or with your shoes more tightly tied.

This is because some people are often prevented or hindered from doing things that other people can do freely, not through any fault of their own, but because of the way society has built structures and systems that disadvantage them.

🔬 Girls might experience sexism – where they are not treated equally to boys. This might mean they are judged more for their appearance or perceived abilities than for what they can actually do, or they are told there are certain things they can't or shouldn't do *because* they're a girl (like playing sport, studying certain subjects or wanting to do a particular job when they grow up). Of course, we know this is completely wrong but it is something that unfortunately still happens.

People whose skin isn't white might experience racism, where others discriminate against them because of how they look or where they are from – for no other reason than that they are different to them. Racism doesn't allow for people to be individuals: it is discrimination based on the belief that people should be defined by how they look, and that they will always think and behave in the same way as everyone else who looks like them. Through history, racism has been the basis for dehumanising people (treating them as less than human) and horrible, often violent discrimination that has done untold damage to those it is targeted against.

✳️ Some disabled or neurodivergent people might experience discrimination that means they have a harder time finding their dream job, and I know there are people who have been told that they won't be able to live a 'normal' life. This isn't true, and these negative assumptions are wrongly based on nothing other than a person's medical diagnosis.

✳️ People who are LGBTQ+ (lesbian, gay, bisexual, trans, queer or of another gender identity or sexual orientation) might experience discrimination where they are bullied or treated badly because of their sexuality, sexual identity and/or their gender identification. People who are gender non-conforming and identify as neither male nor female (which we call non-binary) may find others not taking their identity or pronouns seriously.

This all sounds very shocking and my hope is that you personally never experience any of these things. My dream is that in the future, these forms of discrimination will get less and less common to the point where they hardly exist at all. I'm pretty confident that this is possible, because so many people in your generation are totally brilliant and accepting of everyone – no matter their skin colour, background, gender, sexual orientation or any other part of their identity.

But unfortunately, in the same way that we explored stereotypes in chapter 1, society still often categorises people into groups due to their particular shared characteristics (for example race) and marginalises them so they are deemed as a 'minority' or 'other' group.

This can make it harder for those people to unlock their potential and pursue their dreams in life, simply because the world we are living in accepts some people more easily than others. For some people, even if they are a brilliant Shoe-ey player, the wind never seems to be on their side.

Remember that if you ever experience any of these things, the problem *isn't* with you. You should **CELEBRATE** being your most **DIVERSE, BEAUTIFUL** and **INCREDIBLE** self. What's more, it doesn't mean the world is always going to be this way. Lots of people want to change it, and lots of them are working very hard to do that.

So what can we do to help that process?

Firstly, we can't let it stop or discourage us from reaching our **POTENTIAL**. The most important part of unlocking our potential is still the things we do and the work we put in. Never forget that. The things you do matter so much more than the actions of people who treat you badly or don't take you seriously. You need to go out with confidence, live your life, and don't let anyone get in your way.

Secondly, we should be **AWARE** of inequality and injustice, especially if it is happening to someone else. Maybe you are someone who faces these problems in your everyday life, or maybe you do not. But I can almost guarantee that you know people who *do* experience this kind of discrimination, even if you haven't seen it with your own eyes.

You might not be able to stop this from happening, as just one person in a big and confusing world, but that doesn't mean you can't do *anything*. You can talk to your friends, stick up for them and ask if there is anything you can do to help. Being a good 'ally' for those who are different or facing difficulties is a superpower in itself. Finding ways to educate yourself, especially by reading experiences people have chosen to share (rather than asking people you know to talk about things that may be upsetting for them), is an important part of this.

Even knowing and recognising that discrimination happens is a step in the right direction. We're better people when we realise that not everyone experiences the world like we do. We're better when we learn that, for some people, there are invisible or unspoken barriers that we don't face – things that make it harder for them to kick their shoes as far as we can.

So, as you are thinking about your own potential, the things you want to get better at and the dreams you want to pursue, remember that it isn't all about you. There are so many other people in your life with their own wants, needs and problems. There is no point in sprinting ahead if it means leaving everyone else behind.

The things you do to help and support them are just as important as – and sometimes *more* important than – the ones you do to help yourself.

Because we have only really fulfilled our potential when everyone around us has had the chance to do the same.

CHAPTER 10

PERFECTLY NEW: WHAT ANIMAL MIGRATION TEACHES US ABOUT COPING WITH CHANGE

Most of the things we have talked about in this book relate to the life you are living now: going to school, seeing friends at the weekend, doing homework, playing sport, arguing with your siblings, helping with the washing up.

That gives you plenty to be thinking about already, and you probably feel like your plate is full enough, thank you very much, without me adding anything else on to it.

But since this is our last chapter together, I want to look forward, towards the future and how your life is going to change.

Because, whether you like it or not, this is going to happen. You will move to a new school, and eventually beyond school altogether. You will make new friends (while hopefully staying in touch with some of your old ones). You'll try new foods, visit new places and do new things. You'll learn about the world – and yourselves. You'll even, eventually, leave home.

That sounds like a lot of **CHANGE** because it is. Our entire life is one big process of growth and evolution. We literally grow up as our bodies reach their full, adult size. And we grow up in all sorts of different ways: our abilities develop, our tastes and interests change, our ambitions and life goals become clearer.

Change can be scary, but it's also **IMPORTANT**. We grow and develop as individuals by meeting new people and learning new things (whether skills or new pieces of knowledge). To do that, we have to put ourselves in situations that we might find difficult at first – like going to a new school or joining a new club.

Let me reassure you that these feelings don't go away as an adult. Grown-ups get scared too about having to try new things and meet people for the first time.

But if we embrace that fear and grab hold of that change, great things can happen. We are at our most alive when having to deal with new things that force us to think and learn.

It probably won't surprise you to hear that dealing with change was something I found difficult growing up. As someone who was (and still is) reliant on routines to make me feel comfortable, new situations could unbalance me. I didn't know where things were, or what was going to happen next. I never knew when a nasty new colour or smell might make my eyes start to water and my head fill with the noise of alarm bells.

But that was only half the story, because new things also *fascinated* me. Even at a young age, I loved to **EXPLORE** and **DISCOVER** equally as much as I feared the unknown. The scientist in me wanted to study new places and environments, making mental maps of them like an explorer.

At the same time, another part of me wanted to run back to somewhere safe and familiar.

I think we all feel a bit like this, our emotions pulling us in opposite directions when we are faced with change. We feel both scared and excited at the same time. It might be terrible, but it could also be great. We'll never know until we try.

Whatever mix of emotions we feel, change is something we must all learn to cope with as our lives develop. Trying new things is one of the **BEST**, most difficult and most important things that any of us will do – and it's something we will *keep doing* at every stage of our lives.

It's also important to remember that we're **NOT** alone in this.

If you think our growth and development as humans is daunting, then spare a thought for animals. Because if starting a new school sounds scary, just wait until you hear about what some of the world's best-travelled animals get up to.

They are *migratory*, which means they move around as the seasons change to find a more suitable habitat: one where there is more food, better shelter and a place for them to have babies.

There are migratory birds, fish and mammals that travel thousands of miles every **YEAR** (or few years) of their lives for this purpose. And in doing so, they go all over the world, to dangerous places and into the territory of other animals that may be their predators (who want to eat them, and often do).

Animal migration is one of the great wonders of our planet. In this final chapter, we will explore these migrations, why they happen and what they can teach us about how to deal with change and adversity in our own lives.

MIGRATION, NOT VACATION

For humans, travelling hundreds or even thousands of miles might be the reason for a particularly exciting holiday.

But for the animals who undergo migrations of a similar distance, it's a lot more serious. They're not packing swimming trunks and sunscreen for a week on the beach. They are beginning journeys that are a matter of life or death: they *need* to go in order to stay alive, but the journey is so perilous that they are risking death to make it.

If it's so dangerous, you might be thinking, then why go in the first place?

Well, in very simple terms, they are doing it for the same reason that you sometimes get up from the sofa and go to the kitchen to get a snack or glass of water. Or the reason that you go to your bedroom at night to sleep.

They migrate because it is their only way of finding food and shelter as the seasons change.

We probably don't think too much about these things: if we are lucky, there is always food in the fridge when we are hungry and a warm bed to sleep in at night.

But imagine if it took you weeks or months to get from one room of your house to another, and if there were suddenly other people in your way trying to steal your food and drag away your duvet.

That may start to give you an idea of what some animals experience not once in their lives but, in most cases, every single year. (Only some wild animals migrate, so you don't need to worry about your family pet leaving for an exciting trip across the desert anytime soon.)

A good example is the migration of the wildebeest (a type of antelope found in parts of Africa), one of the biggest and most famous of these journeys. You'll know about it if you've seen *The Lion King*, where the wildebeest migration features in a rather important scene (no spoilers!).

Wildebeest are constantly on the move between two main habitats: the Serengeti in Tanzania and the Masai Mara in Kenya. They go back and forth, year after year, towards where the grass is growing and the water flowing.

This migration is a massive event. It involves around **1.5 MILLION** animals: mostly wildebeest but also some antelope and zebra. Around a third of that number are baby wildebeest that have just been born, but that develop within days to run as quickly as their mothers.

It's a journey of several hundred miles, which sadly will be too far for some. Each year, many wildebeest will be eaten by predators such as lions, hyenas and cheetahs. Others will die of exhaustion or starvation, or drown while crossing deep rivers on the route.

Around 250,000 wildebeest who begin the migration north each spring will not survive the journey. But those who do, and who keep on surviving, can live to see as many as twenty of these extraordinary journeys in their lives.

The baby wildebeest that follows its mother for hundreds of miles across the savannah (grassland) will grow up to become the parent that leads its own children on the same extraordinary journey. It's an amazing example of survival, growth and development.

Now, we might not have to follow in those exact footsteps. The good news is that no one is asking you to swim across river rapids or try to outrun a cheetah before breakfast.

But we *can* look to migration and start living a little bit more like an animal when it comes to coping with change in our own lives, less dramatic and dangerous though it might be.

HOW TO FIND YOUR INNER WILDEBEEST

- Step one: accept that change is **NECESSARY**. Embrace the new and scary things in your life – whether it's getting used to a new school, meeting new people or trying new food that might just become your next favourite meal. These new things are as important to our growth and development as migration is to the survival of animals in the wild. These 'leaps' are the way we learn, develop and grow. These things only happen when we embrace the uncertainty and excitement of something new with the same courage and commitment of the wildebeest setting out on its annual journey of migration.

 Step two: remember that humans are **GOOD AT DEALING WITH CHANGE**, even though we often don't think that we are. Humans are surprisingly good at adapting to new conditions and dealing with struggles in our lives. Like when, during a global pandemic, you had to do all of your school lessons at home via video call – you see, don't tell me you're not seriously good at adapting! Of course, we all have our limits and things that push our physical and mental health to breaking point, but it's also true that most of us can 'deal' with more than we would ever expect, and that difficult experiences help us to evolve.

Migratory animals are the same. Their bodies are equipped with all sorts of neat tricks to help them manage these long, difficult journeys. For one, they don't get lost, even though you will never see a wildebeest consulting a map or checking satnav. Instead, animals have their own 'inbuilt' systems. The wildebeest use their sense of smell to follow the scent of rain, the best clue about where the grass they are searching for will be growing. Some fish are moved around by strong ocean currents known as *gyres* (ji-uhrs) that act a bit like a seaborne conveyor belt. Birds and fish can also use the earth's magnetic field to move themselves in the right direction. This is so accurate that the Atlantic salmon, which swims thousands of miles from river to ocean and back (this takes it a couple of years) can actually find its way back not just to the same river it was born in, but almost the *exact same spot* where it first came from. Pretty cool!

The lesson? Animals are extremely well adapted to deal with the harsh environments they must survive during migration. As humans, we are very well adjusted for change too.

If you want the evidence, look at how we have evolved as a species over millions of years of history: moving around the world and learning to walk, make tools, set fires and build shelters. These were all very important processes of evolution that have helped bring us to the world we live in today.

This series of giant leaps has made humanity the dominant animal species on the planet and put us at the top of the food chain. If you're interested, look up something called the **ANTHROPOCENE**: the scientific term for the era in which humans have had a significant impact on the planet, one some believe started fifteen thousand years ago.

Human evolution shows that we have constantly developed as a species through our history, adapting to the world around us and developing new skills and abilities along the way. It's what has taken human beings from living in forests and caves to the highly advanced cities of the twenty-first century. (I hear that the Wi-Fi in the Stone Age was pretty slow.)

We can all take a little reassurance from that, about our own ability to evolve and develop in much smaller ways. If the first step to coping with change is to accept its importance, then the second is to believe in our ability to cope with that change – to emerge stronger, even if the journey may be difficult.

BACKWARD AND FORWARD, SIDE TO SIDE

The migration of animals can teach us lots about how to deal with change and the challenges it will throw at us.

It also carries one final lesson: not all change is permanent, or takes us in a single direction.

Remember that our wildebeest end up back where they started, on the Serengeti. They go through that amazing journey, and take all those massive risks, just so they can survive to get back to the beginning again. They are back where they began, but that doesn't mean they haven't changed in all sorts of important ways.

I think that has something in common with our own development and evolution as people.

Because yes, we are changing, developing and becoming more advanced as human beings throughout our lives.

And as we do that, our environment keeps changing too, until we become grown-ups with a home, a life and maybe a family of our own.

But as we experience all that change, a part of us is also staying where it was, or going back to where we started.

⚛ Making new friends doesn't mean we are going to lose the ones we have now. Some of our most valuable relationships in life will be with the people we have known the longest, although the circumstances of life will also mean we can't stay friends with everyone for ever.

✱ Finding new hobbies and interests doesn't mean we have to give up on the ones we enjoy now. One day, you will look back at some of the things you are doing now and think they were childish and a bit silly. But in other hobbies and passions, you will recognise the beginnings of something that has become a massive part of your life – like early science experiments were for me, showing me that it was how I wanted to spend my life. The fun (or frustrating) part is that you won't know until later which is which!

ASK A PARENT OR TRUSTED ADULT WHICH OF THEIR HOBBIES OR PASSIONS FROM CHILDHOOD THEY STILL CARE ABOUT TODAY.

I say all this because life is complicated, and we don't always know which direction we will end up going in. We know that there will be lots of change, but it isn't always clear whether that is taking us forward in a

straight line or around in a circle. We don't always know which bits of us are going to change for ever and which will stay the same.

In the end, we need a mix of both these things: the danger and excitement of the new and the comfort and familiarity of the old. We will have times in our lives when we bravely forge forward into the unknown, and others when we look to our past for clues about what to do next. Both can be part of our growth and development: it's not a contradiction to move forward at the same time as looking backward.

All of this is part of life's rich and colourful tapestry, one that is in your hands to weave, with the wonderful tools of science at your disposal.

I wish you luck on your journey. I know it's going to be a great and wonderful adventure. Like the wildebeest and the salmon, you're going to go to the most wonderful places, see the most amazing things and have the most brilliant time.

Have fun! (And don't forget to pack your umbrella.)

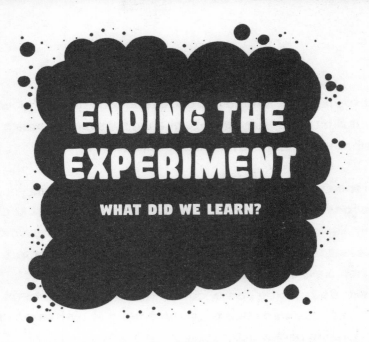

ENDING THE EXPERIMENT

WHAT DID WE LEARN?

So this is it. Our journey **TOGETHER** is coming to an end.

It's taken us through many of the weird and wonderful parts of life, and many of the most **BRILLIANT** and **BEAUTIFUL** bits of science.

We've learned how to use the weather to manage our emotions, how to find a natural habitat that is all our own and how to use plants as a template for pursuing our passions.

We've explored the extraordinary work of stem cells inside the human body, the awe-inspiring journeys of migratory animals and the amazing unseen power of forces to shape our world.

We've let computers teach us how to be more confident (but not *too* confident!) and had science show us how to have more productive disagreements.

I hope the ideas in this book will be useful to you as you go forward in the big adventure of growing up.

And I hope this is just the beginning of your exploration of science as a guide to this amazing world we live in.

Every topic we have covered in this book is just scratching the surface. These are subjects you could read hundreds of books about without knowing everything there is to know.

So I'm keeping my fingers crossed that you might read a few more and discover how much science has to teach us (I am still learning this too!). It's a great thing to have the tools, but the real magic happens when you start using what you have learned to build your own tools and take leaps of faith to live life.

As well as scientific ideas, I hope you will also take away some ideas for life: ones that can help you with the ups and downs you will experience.

Although we've covered a lot of different topics in this book, there are also some themes that most of them have in common. Here are a few I hope we've learned together:

 DIFFERENCE is precious. We are all individuals and no one else looks, thinks or behaves exactly the same as we do. No one has had the exact same life experience. Each one of us is unique: a complete one-off. We should love ourselves as individuals: the person we really are and the person only we can be. And we should *also* embrace everyone else's individuality: their differences and their uniqueness. We have so much to learn from them, as they do from us.

It is the coming together of all these different ways of living, thinking and being that makes life so interesting. Don't ever feel bad for being different, and don't ever try to make anyone else feel bad because they are. Conformity is boring, and difference is beautiful. So embrace it!

 Our differences, and our individuality, don't mean we are meant to be alone in this life. We need to **WORK TOGETHER** to achieve brilliant things. We are so much stronger when playing in a team, whether on the sports field, doing a class project or getting through the washing up as quickly as possible.

I hope the science in this book shows the true power of teamwork. Think of all those different cells in your body, working together in perfect harmony to keep you alive. Think of the wildebeest migration, done in that massive team of more than a million animals. The natural world is trying to tell us something: we need other people to help us, and we need to be a helper to them too. It is this togetherness that helps us all to move forward in life.

Finally, never forget that **KINDNESS** matters. We've talked so much in this book about being kind to yourself: accepting the way you are and the things you enjoy doing, not trying to hide these things away or pretending to be someone else. And we've talked about being kind to other people: understanding how they may see the world differently from you, and having empathy with how they experience life in their own way.

This may sound obvious, but it's also difficult to put into practice. It's incredibly easy to be a harsh judge: to ask why people can't just think the same way you do, or to join in the laughter at the person who finishes last.

It's a lot more *difficult* to actually stop, understand someone's personal situation and work out if there is anything you can do to help them. That is kindness, compassion and empathy. And the really brave people in life are the ones who find ways to show these things, and who make it a priority to look out for and support other people.

Those are my big lessons from writing this book. I'm sure you will have some more of your own. So write them down, talk about them and come back in a year's time to see if you have changed your mind about anything.

Remember, just like science, life is a great experiment. **NEVER** be afraid to try things. Keep working to **DISCOVER** more about yourself, other people and the world around you. And don't forget that, when you need it, science will always be there for **YOU**.

ACKNOWLEDGEMENTS

Where do I start? I'd like to thank my younger siblings – Tiger Ramsey, Lilly Pang and Agatha Pang – and my cousins – Lola, Ruby and Matilda Parkes – for their market research and honest feedback that helped me frame this book. All of them provided me with an incredible insight into how inquisitive young minds are and how much they have to offer this world. I'd like to thank my mum Sonia, dad Peter and sister Lydia, who helped with material for this book by providing anecdotes and insight into their lived experience in raising a neurodiverse child. I'd like to thank Uncle Mike and Uncle John, my science sidekicks, who have always questioned my thoughts, for permanently lending me their science books which inspired my whole career. I am forever grateful to call them family.

I'd also like to thank the teachers and mentors who believed in me, supported me and let me get on with doing what I loved without judgement – Michelle Middleton, Alison Banyard, Clare Welham, Leslie Morris, Dr Keith Rose, Margie Burnet-Ward, Steve Hubbard, Roy Royston, Ed Jenkins and Chris Swain.

I'd like to thank Laurène Boglio, who created the wonderful illustrations you see throughout the book. Thank you to the Hachette team, who invited me to make this book and helped it come to life: Laura Horsley, Kaltoun Yusuf, Victoria Walsh, Samuel Perrett and Pippi Grantham-Wright; and to my agent Adam Gauntlett and editorial sidekick Josh Davis.

RESOURCES

Here are some additional resources that you might find helpful:

National Autistic Society www.autism.org.uk
A central resource for supporting autistic individuals in life, work and functioning in society.

ADHD Foundation www.adhdfoundation.org.uk
A great resource for living and working with ADHD. They even have a comic on neurodiversity at school!

Lightyear Foundation www.lightyearfoundation.org
Science support for special education needs.

In2scienceUK www.in2scienceuk.org
A science charity specifically supporting students from under-represented communities and marginalised demographics.

There are also lots of great writers, illustrators and activists out there too. I'd recommend reading Abigail Balfe's *A Different Sort of Normal* and looking up the amazing 21andsensory blog: www.21andsensory.wordpress. com. If your older siblings or parents have Instagram, they can show you 21andsensory's amazing illustrations online too.

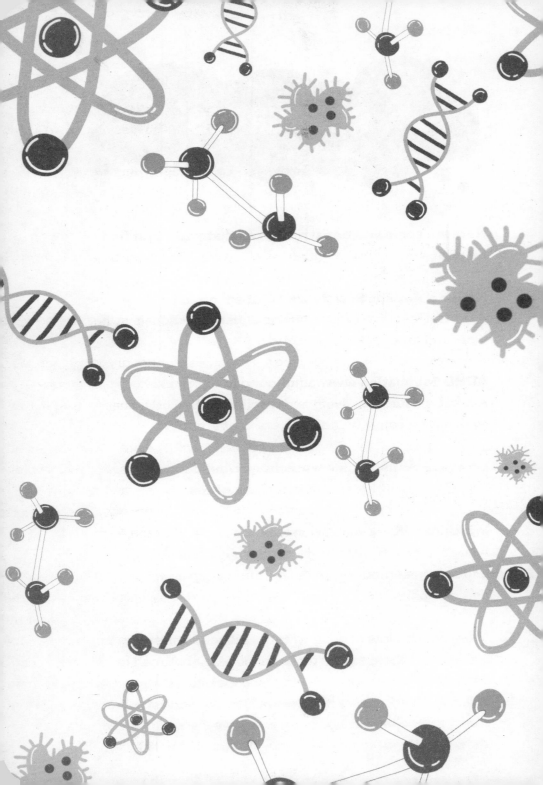